Talk Time

Everyday English Conversation

Student Book 2

D1500620

Susan Stempleski

OXFORD

UNIVERSITY PRESS

OXFORD
UNIVERSITY PRESS

198 Madison Avenue
New York, NY 10016 USA

Great Clarendon Street, Oxford OX2 6DP UK

Oxford University Press is a department of the University of Oxford.
It furthers the University's objective of excellence in research, scholarship,
and education by publishing worldwide in

Oxford   New York

Auckland   Cape Town   Dar es Salaam   Hong Kong   Karachi
Kuala Lumpur   Madrid   Melbourne   Mexico City   Nairobi
New Delhi   Shanghai   Taipei   Toronto

With offices in

Argentina   Austria   Brazil   Chile   Czech Republic   France   Greece
Guatemala   Hungary   Italy   Japan   Poland   Portugal   Singapore
South Korea   Switzerland   Thailand   Turkey   Ukraine   Vietnam

OXFORD and OXFORD ENGLISH are registered trademarks of
Oxford University Press.

© Oxford University Press 2007

Database right Oxford University Press (maker)

Library of Congress Cataloging-In-Publication Data

Stempleski, Susan.
    Talk time: student book / Susan Stempleski.
      p. cm.
    Contents: — [1] Book 1 — [2] Book 2 — [3] Book 3.
    ISBN: 978-0-19-438201-4 (Student bk. 1)
    ISBN: 978-0-19-438208-3 (Student bk. 2)
    ISBN: 978-0-19-438217-5 (Student bk. 3)
    1. English language—Textbooks for foreign speakers. 2. English language—
Grammar—Problems, exercises, etc. I. Title

PE1128.S743 2006
428.2'4–dc22

                                        2006040020

No unauthorized photocopying

All rights reserved. No part of this publication may be reproduced, stored
in a retrieval system, or transmitted, in any form or by any means, without
the prior permission in writing of Oxford University Press, or as expressly
permitted by law, or under terms agreed with the appropriate copyright
clearance organization. Enquiries concerning reproduction outside the scope
of the above should be sent to the ELT Rights Department, Oxford University
Press, at the address above.

You must not circulate this book in any other binding or cover and you must
impose this same condition on any acquirer.

Any websites referred to in this publication are in the public domain and
their addresses are provided by Oxford University Press for information only.
Oxford University Press disclaims any responsibility for the content.

Market Development Director, Asia: Chris Balderston
Senior Editor: Patricia O'Neill
Art Director: Maj-Britt Hagsted
Senior Designer: Stacy Merlin
Art Editor: Elizabeth Blomster
Photo Editor: Justine Eun
Production Manager: Shanta Persaud
Production Controller: Zainaltu Jawat Ali

ISBN: 978 0 19 438208 3 (Student Book)
ISBN: 978 0 19 439291 4 (Student Book with CD)

Printed in China

10 9 8

This book is printed on paper from certified and well- managed sources.

ACKNOWLEDGMENTS

Stills photography by: Dennis Kitchen Studio, 64, 87

Illustrations by: Illustrations by: Barbara Bastian. pp. 6, 18, 21, 31, 36, 57, 60, 69, 74;
Kathy Baxindale pp.24, 27, 72; Richard Deverell pp.34, 37, 46; Jody Emery pp.31,
33, 45, 48, 73; Janos Jatner/Beehive Illustration pp.7, 64; Katie Mac/NB Illustration
Ltd. pp.2, 5, 11, 71; Marc Monés/American Artists pp.14, 23, 56, 62; Pulsar Studio/
Beehive Illustration pp.28, 38, 61, 66, 76 ; Marco Schaaf/NB Illustration Ltd. pp.17,
65, 67; Rob Schuster pp.30, 39, 54; William Waitzman pp.8, 32, 47, 63, 75, 84;
Tracey Wood/Reactor Art & Design pp.12, 19, 41, 43, 58

We would like to thank the following for their permission to reproduce photographs: Age
footstock: Vstock LLC, 68; Alamy: Aflo Foto Agency, 4 (soccer); Peter Barrit, 13
(Van Gogh); blickwinkel, 25 (zoo); Judith Collins, 42 (camera); David R. Frazier
Photolibrary, Inc., 22 (art museum); Mary-Kate Denny, 53; Dinodia Images, 13
(Gandhi); Justine Eun/OUP, 40; face to face Bildagentur GmbH, 87 (apple); FAN
travelstock, 25 (dance club); Steve Hamblin, 42 (ATM); D. Hurst, 42 (laptop);
imagebroker, 25 (concert); ImageState, 25 (baseball); Janine Wiedel Photolibrary,
4 (subway), 25 (art museum); NORMA JOSEPH, 49 (stamp collector); eddie linssen,
44; Mary Evans Picture Library, 13 (DaVinci); Nordicphotos, 25 (golf), 55 (skiing);
POPPERFOTO, 13 (Marie Curie, Martin Luther King, Jr.), 25 (soccer); Trevor
Smithers ARPS, 55 (guided tour); Stock Connection Distribution, 52 (boxing),
55 (hikers); Peter Stroumtsos, 87 (soup); Peter Titmuss, 55 (tour bus); David
Young-Wolff, 50; CORBIS: Randy Faris, 22 (friends); Diego Giudice, 55 (walking
tour); John Henley, 10 (graduate); Robbie Jack, 70 (dancers); Viviane Moss, 1 (web
designer); Chuck Savage, 4 (students); Virgo/zefa, 49 (cards player); Gerald Cubitt:
16 (Aukland), 55 (cruise); Dennis Kitchen Studios: 64, 87 (fish); Getty Images:
Getty Images News, 15 (Princess Diana); Getty Images Sports, 49 (trading cards);
Tony Hopewell/The Image Bank, 49 (board game); Hulton Archive, 13 (Charlie
Chaplin, 15 (Napoleon, Picasso, Marie Curie, Frida Kahlo); David Samuel Robbins/
Photographer's Choice, 42 (TV); ImageState: First Light, 42 (sofa); foodfolio,
42 (plant); RubberBall, 52 (lifting weights); Inmagine: Bananastock, 1 (chef), 4
(lunch), 29, 55 (backpacking); Designpics, 26; Ingram Publishing, 1 (teacher), 87
(cookies); Inspirestock, 1 (architect); Mixa, 59; Photodisc, 42 (mp3 player); Pixtal,
10 (surprised); Jupiterimages Unlimited: Bananastock, 52 (ping-pong); Brand X
Pictures, 42 (traffic light, banana); Comstock, 42 (bicycle); Creatas, 1 (musician), 49
(chess player); Thinkstock, 32, 42 (airplane); THE KOBAL COLLECTION:
PARAMOUNT/SEAKWOOD, JOHN, 70 (female director); TOHO/KUROSAWA, 13
(Akira Kurosawa); Masterfile: Burazin, 87 (microwave); Peter Griffith, 87 (woman
with pie); Carlo Hindian, 1 (dentist); Robert Karpa, 1 (actor); Mark Liebowitz,
22 (sightseeing), 55 (train travel); Omni-Photo Communications: Phil Mislinski,
57 (surfer); Paul Slaughter, 25 (surfer); Oxford University Press: Justine Eun, 40
(woman with scarf, woman with sweater); Photo Edit, Inc.: Spencer Grant, 35,
52 (karate); Bonnie Kamin, 47; Dennis MacDonald, 70 (drawing a portrait); Phil
Martin, 49 (jigsaw puzzle); Felicia Martinez, 52 (yoga); Michael Newman, 25
(picnic); Dwayne Newton, 4 (surfing the web); Dana White, 49 (comics); Colin
Young-Wolff, 42 (jeans); Photographersdirect.com: Kari Erik Martilla Photography,
42 (shorts); Lino Wchima Photography, 70 (singer); Punchstock: Bananastock, 29,
55 (bus tour); bilderlounge, 40 (man in tie); Blend Images, 10 (bored), 22 (reading),
49 (web surfer); Brand X Pictures, 22 (movies); CORBIS, 1 (computer programmer),
42 (piano); Digital Vision, 1 (pilot); fStop, 40 (woman in skirt), 52 (wrestling); Image
Source, 10 (arguing, nervous), 25 (café); Medioimages, 55 (beach); PhotoAlto, 1
(accountant); Photodisc, 1 (tour guide), 42 (wastebasket, hotdog, socks, guitar,
boots, t-shirt), 70 (composing music); Purestock, 42 (chicken); RubberBall, 42
(cell phone); Stockbyte, 4 (couple), 22 (camping), 40 (man in t-shirt), 42 (cat), 87
(eating cereal); Stockdisc, 42 (taxi), 49 (guitar player); Sergio Piumatti: 70 (actors);
SuperStock: age fotostock, 1 (saleswoman), 15 (Nefertiti), 16 (Singapore, Mexico
City, New York City, Kyoto), 20, 49 (baseball caps, snowboarder), 55 (rafting);
John Arnold, 74 (skiing); Food Collection, 42 (egg); Lisette Le Bon, 10 (spectators);
National Portrait Gallery, 13 (Elizabeth I); Photononstop, 87 (salt being added
to pot); Prisma, 55 (skiers, passenger train); Kurt Scholz, 25 (play performance);
SuperStock, Inc., 13 (Queen Victoria), 15 (Mozart, Genghis Khan), 25 (dancers);
Yoshio Tomii. 16 (Paris); Underwood Photo Archives, 13 (Albert Einstein).

*We would like to thank the following for their permission to reproduce photographs on the
cover:* Getty Images (couple); Background Images: Corbis (clock); Getty Images
(group of four teens).

The publishers would like to thank the following for their help in developing this series: Mei-ho
Chiu, Taiwan; Kirsten Duckett, Seoul, South Korea; Laura MacGregor, Tokyo, Japan;
Grant Warfield, Seoul, South Korea; Andrew Zitzmann, Osaka, Japan.

The publishers would also like to thank the following OUP staff for their support and assistance:
Ted Yoshioka.

Contents

Scope and sequence iv

To the student v

1 Jobs 1

Daily activities 4

2 Current activities 7

Feelings 10

3 People we admire 13

Cities 16

4 On the weekend 19

On vacation 22

5 Entertainment 25

Music 28

6 A city square 31

Public transportation 34

7 At a supermarket 37

Clothes and colors 40

8 Shops and stores 43

Places around town 46

9 Hobbies 49

Indoor exercise 52

10 Travel plans 55

Trip preparations 58

11 Quantities 61

Cooking 64

12 Job skills 67

Artistic talents 70

Communication task: Student B pages 73

Check your English 77

Key vocabulary 89

Scope and sequence

Unit	Theme	Grammar	Vocabulary
1 page 1	Jobs Daily activities	*Wh-* questions in the simple present; Yes/No questions in the simple present	Different types of jobs; everyday activities
2 page 7	Current activities Feelings	The present continuous; object pronouns	Current activities; feelings and emotions
3 page 13	People we admire Cities	Simple past of *be*; past time expressions; *Wh-* questions with the simple past of *be*	Famous and notable people; popular cities with descriptions, adjectives
4 page 19	On the weekend On vacation	The simple past; questions in the simple past	Weekend activities; things to do while on vacation
5 page 25	Entertainment Music	The future with *be going to* and present continuous; invitations and suggestions	Types of entertainment, recreational activities; types of music
6 page 31	A city square Public transportation	Prepositions of place; indirect questions	Things in a city; types of public transportation
7 page 37	At a supermarket Clothes and colors	*How many/how much*; Preferences; comparative of adjectives	Items in a supermarket; types of clothing, different colors
8 page 43	Shops and stores Places around town	Giving directions; Prepositions of direction	Types of stores; buildings and places in town
9 page 49	Hobbies Indoor exercise	Verb + infinitive; verb + noun	Things to collect, things to play, things to do; indoor sports
10 page 55	Travel plans Trip preparations	Future plans with *be going to* and *will*; *like to* versus *would like to*	Things to do while traveling; what to do before going on a trip
11 page 61	Quantities Cooking	*A … of …* ; imperatives for instructions; sequence markers	Amounts: a bag, a cup, a spoonful; kitchen activities
12 page 67	Job skills Artistic talents	Using *can* and *know how to* for ability; using *could* for ability in the past	Abilities needed for specific jobs; types of artistic talents

To the student

Welcome to *Talk Time*. Let's take a look at a unit.

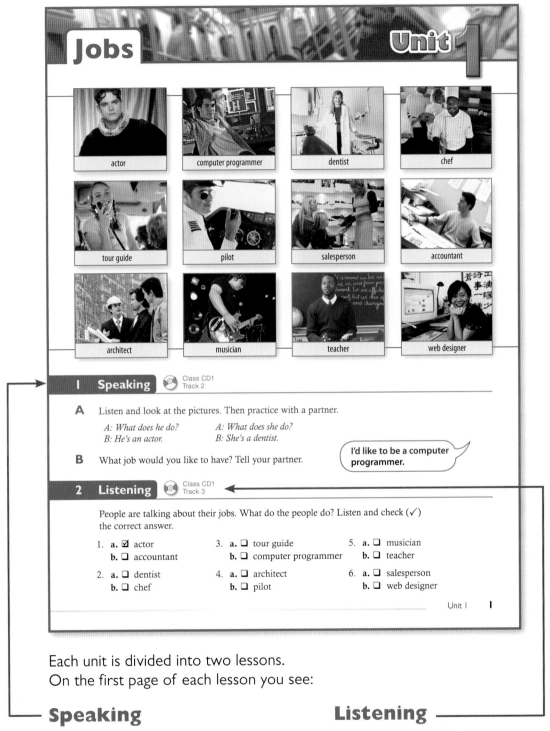

Each unit is divided into two lessons.
On the first page of each lesson you see:

Speaking

First you practice the new vocabulary for this lesson. You will listen to the CD and look at the pictures. Then you practice using the new words with a classmate.

Listening

In this section, you listen to the vocabulary in short conversations and answer some questions.

On the second page of each lesson you see:

Grammar

In this section, you see the grammar focus for this lesson. You listen to the CD and then practice the grammar.

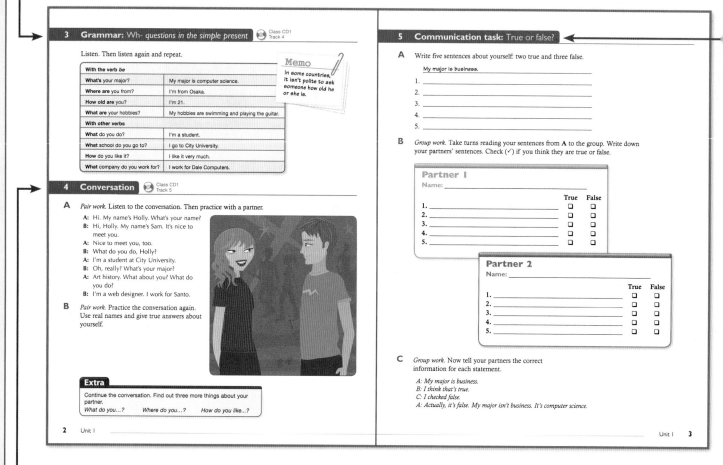

On the third page of each lesson you see:

Conversation

In this section, you listen to a conversation and then practice with a partner. This lets you practice the vocabulary and grammar of the lesson in a larger context. It also lets you use your own information.

Communication task

In this section, you practice the language of the lesson with a partner or a small group. This section lets you use your own information to speak more freely about the topic. Sometimes you and your partner will look at the same page, and sometimes you will look at different pages.

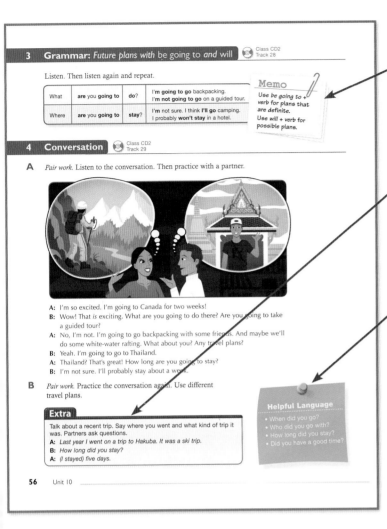

Other things you see in the unit:

Memo

The *Memo* reminds you about rules of English that are different from your language, for example, contractions. The language in the Memo will help you complete the activities.

Extra

Sometimes you will see an *Extra* activity. This lets you practice more with the same language from the activity.

Helpful Language

The Helpful Language note gives you questions or phrases that will help you complete the activities. They provide cues you can use to keep talking longer with your partner.

CD Icon

The CD icon tells you that this activity is recorded on the audio CD, and your teacher may play it in class in order for you to do the activity.

Check your English

At the back of the book, there is a review page called *Check your English*. This page gives you a chance to review the language from the unit.

Every lesson gives you time to listen to English and time to talk with your classmates. *Talk Time* will help you increase your vocabulary and improve grammatical accuracy. I hope you enjoy studying with *Talk Time*. Good luck!

Jobs

actor

computer programmer

dentist

chef

tour guide

pilot

salesperson

accountant

architect

musician

teacher

web designer

1 Speaking
Class CD1
Track 2

A Listen and look at the pictures. Then practice with a partner.

A: *What does he do?*   A: *What does she do?*
B: *He's an actor.*   B: *She's a dentist.*

B What job would you like to have? Tell your partner.

> I'd like to be a computer programmer.

2 Listening
Class CD1
Track 3

People are talking about their jobs. What do the people do? Listen and check (✓) the correct answer.

1. **a.** ☑ actor
   b. ☐ accountant

2. **a.** ☐ dentist
   b. ☐ chef

3. **a.** ☐ tour guide
   b. ☐ computer programmer

4. **a.** ☐ architect
   b. ☐ pilot

5. **a.** ☐ musician
   b. ☐ teacher

6. **a.** ☐ salesperson
   b. ☐ web designer

3 Grammar: Wh- *questions in the simple present*
Class CD1
Track 4

Listen. Then listen again and repeat.

With the verb *be*	
What's your major?	My major is computer science.
Where are you from?	I'm from Osaka.
How old are you?	I'm 21.
What are your hobbies?	My hobbies are swimming and playing the guitar.
With other verbs	
What do you do?	I'm a student.
What school do you go to?	I go to City University.
How do you like it?	I like it very much.
What company do you work for?	I work for Dale Computers.

> **Memo**
>
> In some countries, it isn't polite to ask someone how old he or she is.

4 Conversation
Class CD1
Track 5

A   *Pair work.* Listen to the conversation. Then practice with a partner.

> **A:** Hi. My name's Holly. What's your name?
> **B:** Hi, Holly. My name's Sam. It's nice to meet you.
> **A:** Nice to meet you, too.
> **B:** What do you do, Holly?
> **A:** I'm a student at City University.
> **B:** Oh, really? What's your major?
> **A:** Art history. What about you? What do you do?
> **B:** I'm a web designer. I work for Santo.

B   *Pair work.* Practice the conversation again. Use real names and give true answers about yourself.

Extra

Continue the conversation. Find out three more things about your partner.

What do you...?   *Where do you...?*   *How do you like...?*

A   Write five sentences about yourself: two true and three false.

My major is business. _____

1. _____

2. _____

3. _____

4. _____

5. _____

B   *Group work.* Take turns reading your sentences from **A** to the group. Write down your partners' sentences. Check (✓) if you think they are true or false.

Partner 1

Name: _____

		True	False
1.	_____	❑	❑
2.	_____	❑	❑
3.	_____	❑	❑
4.	_____	❑	❑
5.	_____	❑	❑

Partner 2

Name: _____

		True	False
1.	_____	❑	❑
2.	_____	❑	❑
3.	_____	❑	❑
4.	_____	❑	❑
5.	_____	❑	❑

C   *Group work.* Now tell your partners the correct information for each statement.

A: *My major is business.*
B: *I think that's true.*
C: *I checked false.*
A: *Actually, it's false. My major isn't business. It's computer science.*

Daily activities

go for a walk

attend class

have lunch

surf the Internet

take the subway

play sports

6 Speaking
Class CD1
Track 6

A Listen and look at the pictures. Then practice with a partner.

> A: *What are they doing?*
> B: *They're going for a walk.*

B Which activities do you do? Tell your partner.

> **On Sundays I like to go for a walk in the park.**

7 Listening
Class CD1
Track 7

A People are asking about everyday activities. Listen and number the activities from 1 to 6.

___ having lunch   _1_ attending class   ___ playing sports
___ surfing the Internet   ___ going for a walk   ___ taking the subway

B Listen again. Check (✓) the best response.

1. **a.** ❑ From 10:00 to 11:30.
   b. ❑ I like it.

2. **a.** ❑ Where do you go?
   b. ❑ Yes, I do.

3. **a.** ❑ No, I don't.
   b. ❑ That's interesting.

4. **a.** ❑ I do, too.
   b. ❑ Yes. I usually do.

5. **a.** ❑ I never watch it.
   b. ❑ Tennis and golf.

6. **a.** ❑ I never do it.
   b. ❑ No, it's not.

A Listen. Then listen again and repeat.

With the verb *be*		
Are you an actor?	Yes, **I am.**	No, **I'm not.**
Is she a pilot?	Yes, **she is.**	No, **she isn't.** / No, **she's not.**
Are they musicians?	Yes, **they are.**	No, **they aren't.** / No, **they're not.**
With other verbs		
Do you work in Singapore?	Yes, **I do.**	No, **I don't.**
Does he work in a gym?	Yes, **he does.**	No, **he doesn't.**
Do they work at home?	Yes, **they do.**	No, **they don't.**

B *Pair work.* Ask and answer questions with your partner.

Do you work in the city? **Yes, I do.**

9 **Conversation** Class CD1
Track 9

A *Group work.* Listen to the conversation. Then practice with two partners.

A: Sam, this is Niran. He's from Thailand.
B: Nice to meet you, Niran. Are you here on vacation?
C: No, I'm not. I'm a student here.
B: Oh, do you go to City University, too?
C: Yes, I do. Holly and I are in the same class.
B: Oh, is your major art history, too?
C: No, it isn't. My major is film. But I'm really interested in art history.
B: Me, too.

B *Group work.* Practice the conversation again. Use real names and give true answers about yourself.

Extra

Continue the conversation. Find out three more things about your partners.
Do you live in…?   *Do you work in…?*   *Do you major in…?*

A   Look at the information below. Are any of these things true for you?

B   *Class activity.* Walk around the classroom. Use the ideas in the squares to ask your classmates questions. Find someone to answer *yes,* and write that person's name in the square. Get five names in a row and you win!

A: Do you like to watch sports on TV?
B: Yes, I do. / No, I don't. Do you…?

HUMAN BINGO

Likes to watch sports on TV	Doesn't like pizza	Plays a musical instrument	Wears contact lenses	Is left-handed
Is a vegetarian	Listens to classical music	Checks his/her e-mail every morning	Doesn't drink coffee	Has a pet
Takes the subway to school	Likes to cycle	FREE	Lives in an apartment	Gets up at 6:00
Is a good cook	Walks to school	Stays up late every night	Drinks milk at breakfast	Sings in the shower
Likes action movies	Plays soccer on weekends	Has relatives in another country	Goes dancing on weekends	Works out in a gym

Current activities

go to college

live at home

write a paper

study Chinese

take a class

teach at a university

travel

visit one's family

work in a restaurant

1 **Speaking** Class CD1 Track 10

A Listen and look at the pictures. Then practice with a partner.

A: Are they going to college?
B: Yes, they are.

B What are you doing these days? Tell your partner.

> I'm going to college.
> I'm living at home…

2 **Listening** Class CD1 Track 11

People are talking about family and friends. Listen and circle the correct answer.

1. Rachel's sister is going to college / (working) in Chicago.

2. Bob's parents are living / visiting his sister in California.

3. Marta is looking for a job / working in a hotel.

4. Jeff's brother is teaching / studying at a university in Australia.

3 Grammar: *The present continuous*

 Class CD1
Track 12

Listen. Then listen again and repeat.

Are you still living in Bangkok?	Yes, I **am**. / No, I'**m not**.
Is she **going** to college now?	Yes, she **is**. / No, she **isn't**.
Are they **taking** classes this semester?	Yes, they **are**. / No, they **aren't**.
What **are** you **doing** these days?	I'**m teaching** at a high school.
Where **is** he **studying** English?	He'**s taking** a course at the university.
Who **are** they **visiting** in Seoul?	They'**re visiting** friends.

Memo

These verbs are not usually used in the present continuous:
have
know
like
love
want

4 Conversation

 Class CD1
Track 13

A *Pair work.* Listen to the conversation. Then practice with a partner.

A: It's nice to see you again. Are you still going to college?

B: No, I'm not. I'm working in a restaurant. I'm a chef!

A: No kidding. How do you like it?

B: I like it a lot. How about you? What are you doing these days?

A: I'm still in college. I'm studying biology.

B: That's interesting. Where are you living?

A: I'm living right here in the city. How about you?

B: Well, right now I'm living at home with my parents. But I'm looking for an apartment in the city.

B *Pair work.* Practice the conversation again. Give true answers or use your imagination.

Extra

Talk about your family or other people you know. Say what they are doing these days. Your partner asks questions.
A: *My sister is living in Paris. She's going to college.*
B: *What's she studying?*
A: *She's studying art history.*

8 Unit 2

A   *Class activity.* Ask classmates the questions in the chart. Write their names and take short notes about their answers.

Name	What classes are you taking?	Why are you studying English?	Where are you living?	Are you working? What kind of work do you do?

A: *What's your name?*
B: *Reiko.*
A: *What classes are you taking, Reiko?*
B: *I'm taking English and art history.*
A: *And why are you studying English?*
B: *I want to visit Australia.*

B   *Class activity.* Look at the information in your chart. Find classmates with things in common. Introduce them to each other.

A: *Reiko, this is Kazuko. Kazuko, this is Reiko. You have a lot in common.*
B: *Hi, Kazuko. Nice to meet you.*
C: *Nice to meet you, too.*
A: *Kazuko is studying art history.*
B: *No kidding. I'm studying art history, too.*

Feelings

excited

angry

bored

surprised

happy

nervous

6 Speaking
Class CD1
Track 14

A Listen and look at the pictures. Then practice with a partner.

> A: *How do they feel?*
> B: *They're excited.*

B How do you feel right now? Why? Tell your partner.

> I'm happy because today is my birthday.

7 Listening
Class CD1
Track 15

A People are talking about how they feel. Listen and circle the correct answer.

1. Fred is excited / surprised.
2. May is happy / nervous.
3. Min is bored / happy.
4. Sue is angry / bored.

B Listen again. What are the people going to do? Circle the correct answer.

1. Fred is going to ____.
   a. travel with his sister
   b. travel with his brother

2. May is starting ____.
   a. a new job today
   b. college today

3. Min is going to ____.
   a. visit his family tonight
   b. see his girlfriend tonight

4. Sue ____.
   a. wants to go to see a movie
   b. doesn't want to go out

8 Grammar: *Object pronouns* Class CD1 Track 16

A Listen. Then listen again and repeat.

Subject pronouns	Verbs	Objects	Subjects	Verbs	Object pronouns
I	like	Kim's friends.	Kim's friends	like	**me.**
You	see	Junko.	Junko	sees	**you.**
He	knows	Sophie.	Sophie	knows	**him.**
She	loves	Jason.	Jason	loves	**her.**
We	know	the teacher.	The teacher	knows	**us.**
They	love	children.	Children	love	**them.**

B *Pair work.* Make a sentence with a subject and an object. Your partner changes them to subject and object pronouns.

An knows Miki.　　She knows her.

9 Conversation Class CD1 Track 17

A *Pair work.* Listen to the conversation. Then practice with a partner.

A: Hello?

B: Hi, Mia. It's Rick. I'm calling you on my new cell phone. Listen, Ken and I are going to see a movie tonight. Do you want to come with us?

A: Sorry, I can't go with you tonight. I'm going to the library with Tanya. We have a big test tomorrow.

B: Who's Tanya?

A: Tanya's my classmate. She's in my English class. I like her a lot. Hey, maybe we can meet tomorrow. Call me in the morning, OK?

B: OK. I'll call you after ten o'clock.

B *Pair work.* Practice the conversation again. Use different names and information.

Pair work. Look at the pictures. Describe the people in the pictures. Where are they? What are they doing? How do they feel? Why do they feel that way? Use your imagination. Say as much as you can about each person.

A: *Nancy is in an office. She's talking to Joe.*
B: *She isn't happy. She's…*

Extra

Ask and answer questions about the people in the picture. Use *who, what, where, why,* and *how* in your questions.
A: *Who's angry?*
B: *Nancy is (angry).*
A: *Why is she angry?*

People we admire

Akira Kurosawa
Japanese movie director

Elizabeth I
English queen

Marie Curie
Polish scientist

Vincent van Gogh
Dutch artist

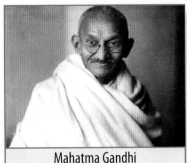
Mahatma Gandhi
Indian leader

Martin Luther King Jr.
American leader

1 Speaking
 Class CD1
Track 18

A Listen and look at the pictures. Then practice with a partner.

> A: Who was Akira Kurosawa?
> B: He was a Japanese movie director.

B Describe a person you admire. Tell your partner about the person.

> I admire Simón Bolívar. We call him *El Libertador*. He was a great leader. He fought for freedom in South America.

2 Listening
 Class CD1
Track 19

People are talking about these famous people. Listen and number the pictures from 1 to 4.

a.

Leonardo da Vinci

b.

Queen Victoria

c.

Albert Einstein

d.

Charlie Chaplin

Listen. Then listen again and repeat.

He **was** born in Paris in 1905.
She **was** a famous writer.
They **were** famous 50 years ago.
Was he born in the United States?   No, he **wasn't**. He **was** born in France.
Were they famous in 1945?   No, they **weren't**. They **were** famous 50 years ago.

Memo

Past time expressions:

last month / summer / year
in 1998

two days / weeks / years ago
a few weeks / months / years ago

A   *Pair work.* Listen to the conversation. Then practice with a partner.

A: Hello?

B: Hi. It's Ben. I called you last night, but you weren't home.

A: I was at the movies.

B: Oh, really? What did you see?

A: *Gandhi.* It's an old movie about Mahatma Gandhi.

B: Was it good?

A: Yeah, the story and the acting were excellent.

B: And what did you learn about Gandhi?

A: Well, he was born in India in 1869. And his real name wasn't
Mahatma Gandhi. It was Mohandas Gandhi.

B: No kidding. Tell me more.

B   *Pair work.* Practice the conversation again. Use different names and information.

A Think of a famous person from the past. The person can be one of the people in
the pictures or some other famous person, real or imaginary.

B *Group work.* Say one sentence about your famous person. *Don't say the person's name.*
Partners ask Yes/No questions to find out who the person is. Take turns.

A: *My famous person was a military leader.*
B: *Was the person a king?*
A: *Yes, he was.*
C: *Was he French?*
A: *No, he wasn't.*
D: *Was he…?*

Napoleon Bonaparte

Mozart

Picasso

Nefertiti

Princess Diana

Marie Curie

Frida Kahlo

Genghis Khan

Extra

Talk about your famous person. Who is the person? Why is the
person famous? What else do you know about the person? Do you
admire him or her? Why or why not?
*My famous person is Pablo Picasso. He was a famous artist. He was
born in Spain. He lived and worked in France. I admire him because
he created many great paintings and sculptures.*

Cities

Singapore
clean / safe / modern

Mexico City
crowded / interesting / beautiful

New York
noisy / exciting / hectic

Paris
charming / romantic / expensive

Auckland
pleasant / quiet / small

Kyoto
historic / fascinating / old

6 Speaking
 Class CD1
Track 22

A Listen and look at the pictures. Then practice with a partner.

> A: What's Singapore like?
> B: It's clean, safe, and modern.

B What is your city or town like? Tell your partner.

> Mexico City is big and crowded.
> It's a very interesting city.

7 Listening
 Class CD1
Track 23

A People are talking about different cities. Listen and number the cities from 1 to 4.

___ Bangkok   ___ London   ___ Quebec City   ___ Ho Chi Minh City

B Listen again. What words do the people use to describe the cities? Check (✓) the correct answers. There is more than one answer for each item.

1. ❑ historic   ❑ clean   ❑ interesting   ❑ safe
2. ❑ small   ❑ crowded   ❑ pleasant   ❑ charming
3. ❑ noisy   ❑ exciting   ❑ expensive   ❑ quiet
4. ❑ modern   ❑ romantic   ❑ safe   ❑ charming

16   Unit 3

A Listen. Then listen again and repeat.

Where were you last week?	**I was** in Kuala Lumpur.
How long were you there?	**I was** there (for) five days.
Why were you there?	**I was** there on vacation.
Who was with you?	My sister and brother **were** with me.
How was the weather?	It **was** wonderful.
What were the people like?	They **were** very friendly.

B *Pair work.* Imagine you and your partner went to two different places last week. Ask your partner questions about where he or she was.

Where were you last week?

I was in New York.

How was...?

9 **Conversation** Class CD1 Track 25

A *Pair work.* Listen to the conversation. Then practice with a partner.

A: Hi, Ron.
B: Oh, hi, Keiko. Where were you last week?
A: I was in San Francisco.
B: San Francisco? Wow! What was it like?
A: Very interesting and charming.
B: How was the food?
A: The food was really good, especially the fish.
B: And what about the weather?
A: The weather was wonderful. It was cool and dry all the time I was there.
B: Sounds good. I'd like to go there.

B *Pair work.* Practice the conversation again. Talk about cities you know.

Extra

Change partners. Practice the conversation with your new partner. Talk about a different city.

A Think about a city you have visited that is special to you. Look at the questions. Make notes in each circle.

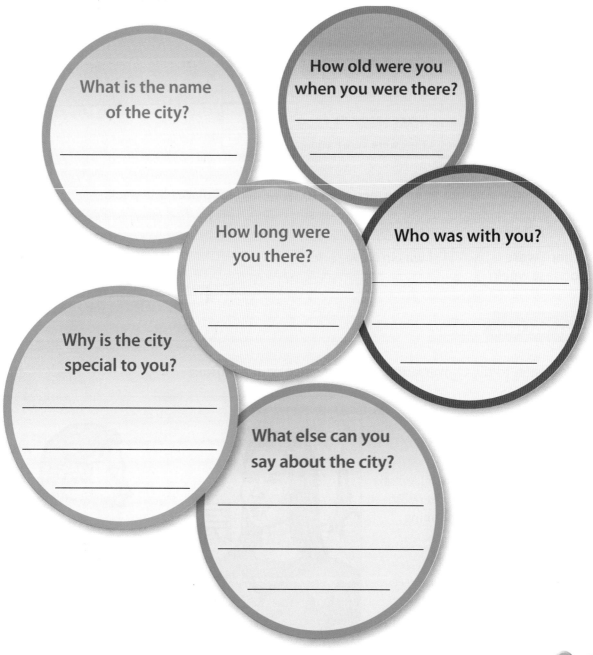

B *Pair work.* Tell your partner about your visit to the city. Partners take notes and ask questions to get more information. Take turns.

C *Class activity.* Tell the class about your partner's special city.

Mei-ling loves Hong Kong. She visited her grandparents there and…

Helpful Language
- Did you meet any people?
- What were they like?
- What about the weather / food / buildings / etc.?

On the weekend

get up late

go to a barbecue

have dinner in a restaurant

go to a karaoke club

get together with friends

meet someone new

drive somewhere

stay home and order a pizza

watch DVDs

play computer games

visit parents

take a nap

1 Speaking
 Class CD1 Track 26

A Listen and look at the pictures. Then practice with a partner.

A: Did she get up late?
B: Yes, she did.

B What did you do last weekend? What didn't you do? Tell your partner.

> I got up late. I didn't go to a barbecue. I…

2 Listening
 Class CD1 Track 27

People are talking about the weekend. What did they do? Listen and number the activities from 1 to 6.

___ watched DVDs   ___ got together with friends   ___ played computer games
___ met someone new   ___ had dinner in a restaurant   ___ went to a karaoke club

Listen. Then listen again and repeat.

Regular verbs	
I **visited** friends.	I **didn't visit** my parents.
You **ordered** pizza.	You **didn't order** salad.
She **watched** TV.	She **didn't watch** DVDs.
We **listened** to music.	We **didn't listen** to the news.

Memo
Notice the spelling:
hate → hated
stop → stopped
study → studied

Irregular verbs	
I **had** dinner at home.	I **didn't have** dinner in a restaurant.
You **went** to a barbecue.	You **didn't go** to a karaoke club.
He **met** someone new.	He **didn't meet** his girlfriend.
We **got up** late.	We **didn't get up** early.

Memo
drive → drove
eat → ate
give → gave
make → made
write → wrote

4 **Conversation** Class CD1 Track 29

A *Pair work.* Listen to the conversation. Then practice with a partner.

A: Hi, Eric. Did you have a nice weekend?
B: Yeah, I had a great weekend.
A: What did you do?
B: Well, on Friday night, a friend came over and we watched DVDs. On Saturday, I got together with friends, and we went to a Mexican restaurant.
A: Was it fun?
B: Oh, yeah. We had a great time. The food was really good, and the restaurant had live music. We stayed there really late.
A: What did you do on Sunday?
B: Not very much. I felt very tired, so I took a long nap.

B *Pair work.* Practice the conversation again. Give true information about yourself.

Extra

Find out three things that you and your partner both did last weekend. Ask questions beginning with *Did you...?* Use the following verbs or any other verbs you know: *meet, visit, do, try, play, take, drive, have, watch.*

A *Pair work.* Did your partner do any of these things last weekend?
Check (✓) your guesses.

Did your partner...

		My guesses		My partner's answers	
		Yes	No	Yes	No
1	watch DVDs on Friday night?	☐	☐	☐	☐
2	get up late on Saturday?	☐	☐	☐	☐
3	meet someone new on Sunday?	☐	☐	☐	☐
4	go to a barbecue on Saturday afternoon?	☐	☐	☐	☐
5	have dinner in a restaurant on Friday?	☐	☐	☐	☐
6	visit his/her parents on Sunday?	☐	☐	☐	☐
7	take a nap on Sunday afternoon?	☐	☐	☐	☐
8	stay home on Saturday morning?	☐	☐	☐	☐
9	get together with friends on Saturday?	☐	☐	☐	☐
10	drive somewhere on Sunday?	☐	☐	☐	☐
11	play computer games on Friday night?	☐	☐	☐	☐
12	go to a karaoke club on Sunday night?	☐	☐	☐	☐

B *Pair work.* Ask your partner questions to check your answers. Partners answer
questions and give one extra piece of information. Take turns.

A: Did you watch DVDs on Friday night?
B: Yes, I did. I watched a science-fiction movie.
A: Did you get up late on Saturday?
B: No, I didn't. I got up at six o'clock.

C *Class activity.* Tell the class about your partner's weekend.

Lin went to a baseball game on Saturday…

On vacation

meet friends

go camping

read a book

go sightseeing

visit museums

see a movie

6 Speaking
Class CD1
Track 30

A Listen and look at the pictures. Then practice with a partner.

A: Did they meet friends?
B: Yes, they did.

B What do you like to do on vacation? What don't you like to do? Tell your partner.

> I like to meet friends. I don't like to go camping. I…

7 Listening
Class CD1
Track 31

A People are talking about vacation activities. Listen and number the activities.

___ went sightseeing   ___ saw movies   ___ met friends
___ visited museums   ___ went camping   ___ read books

B Listen again. Did the people enjoy the activities? Check (✓) *Yes* or *No*.

1. ❑ Yes ❑ No   3. ❑ Yes ❑ No   5. ❑ Yes ❑ No

2. ❑ Yes ❑ No   4. ❑ Yes ❑ No   6. ❑ Yes ❑ No

A Listen. Then listen again and repeat.

Yes/No questions	
Did you **meet** friends?	Yes, I **did**. / No, I **didn't**.
Did she **get up** late?	Yes, she **did**. / No, she **didn't**.
Did they **stay** home?	Yes, they **did**. / No, they **didn't**.
Wh- questions	
What did you **do** on your vacation?	I **stayed** home and **watched** TV.
Where did Nami go?	She **went** to Vietnam.
Who did Chin meet?	He **met** some people from Japan.

B *Pair work.* Ask your partner questions about his or her last vacation.

What did you do on your last vacation?

I visited family in the city.

9 **Conversation**   Class CD1 Track 33

A *Pair work.* Listen to the conversation. Then practice with a partner.

A: So, how did you spend your vacation, Joe?
B: Oh, I had a great time. I went to Australia with my brother.
A: Did you visit Sydney?
B: No, we didn't. We went rock climbing in Victoria. It was really exciting. And a lot of fun. How about you? What did you do on your vacation?
A: I went to Hawaii.
B: Hawaii! That sounds like fun. Did you take a lot of photos?
A: Uh-huh. Do you want to see them?

B *Pair work.* Practice the conversation again. Use your imagination and talk about different places and activities.

A Look at the chart. Use the words at the left to write questions about a vacation.

	Your best vacation	Your partner's best vacation
1 Where / go _Where did you go?_		
2 When / go there		
3 go there / with someone		
4 How long / there		
5 Where / stay		
6 What / do		
7 meet / friendly people		
8 take / photos		

B Think about your best vacation. It can be a vacation you took a long time ago or recently. Make short notes about the vacation in the chart.

C _Pair work._ Ask your partner about his or her best vacation. Take notes and ask questions to get more information. Take turns.

D _Class activity._ Tell the class about your partner's best vacation.

Entertainment

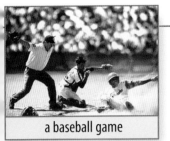
a baseball game

a dance club

a play

an opera

a dance performance

a museum

a picnic

a cafe

a golf tournament

a concert

a soccer match

a zoo

1 Speaking

 Class CD1 Track 34

A Listen and look at the pictures. Then practice with a partner.

A: Are you going to see a baseball game soon?
B: Yes, I am. / No, I'm not.

> I saw a baseball game a month ago. I went to a dance club last week. I…

B When did you last see the things or go to the places in the pictures? Tell your partner.

2 Listening

 Class CD1 Track 35

People are talking about kinds of entertainment. What do they talk about? Listen and check (✓) the correct answer.

1. **a.** ❑ a soccer match
   b. ❑ an opera

2. **a.** ❑ a cafe
   b. ❑ a zoo

3. **a.** ❑ a golf tournament
   b. ❑ a play

4. **a.** ❑ a dance club
   b. ❑ a dance performance

5. **a.** ❑ a museum
   b. ❑ a baseball game

6. **a.** ❑ a concert
   b. ❑ a picnic

3 Grammar: *Future with* be going to *and present continuous*

Listen. Then listen again and repeat.

With *be going to*	
What **are** you **going to do** tonight?	I**'m going to see** a play.
Are you **going to go** to the zoo on Saturday?	Yes, I **am**.
With the present continuous	
What **is** she **doing** on Sunday?	She**'s going** to a golf tournament.
Are they **doing** anything on Friday night?	No, they**'re not**.

Memo
You can use *be going to* or the present continuous to talk about plans.

4 Conversation

A *Pair work.* Listen to the conversation. Then practice with a partner.

A: So, are you doing anything this weekend?

B: Yeah. I'm going to a picnic.

A: Oh, really? Who's going to be there?

B: Well, Adi and Tam are going to go with me.

A: What about Lian?

B: No, she isn't going to be there. She's working all weekend. What about you? What are you doing this weekend?

A: I'm going to go to a golf tournament.

B: A golf tournament? That's interesting.

B *Pair work.* Practice the conversation again. Give true answers or use your imagination.

Extra

Change partners. Practice the conversation again with your new partner.

A   Look at the activities in the chart. Which of these things are you going
to do this week?

B   *Class activity.* Find classmates who are going to do these activities. Ask questions
with *who, where, when, what, why,* or *how* to get more information. Write your
classmates' names and any extra information.

> *A: Min-chul, are you going (to go) to a cafe this week?*
> *B: Yes, I am.*
> *A: When are you going to go?*
> *B: I'm going on Saturday.*
> *A: Who are you going to go with?*
> *B: I'm going with some friends.*

Find a classmate who is going to...	Name	Extra information
go to a cafe	▶	▶
go to a baseball game	▶	▶
go to an opera	▶	▶
go to a dance club	▶	▶
attend a dance performance	▶	▶
visit a museum	▶	▶
have a picnic	▶	▶
see a play	▶	▶
go to a concert	▶	▶
go to a zoo	▶	▶
see a soccer match	▶	▶
watch a golf tournament	▶	▶

C   *Group work.* Tell the group about the information you collected. Tell them as many
details as you can.

> *Min-chul is going to a cafe on Saturday. He's going to go there with friends.*

Music

classical

country and western

hip-hop

jazz

pop

rock

6 Speaking   Class CD1 Track 38

A Listen and look at the pictures. Then practice with a partner.

A: Are you going to listen to classical music tonight?
B: Yes, I am. / No, I'm not.

B What's your favorite kind of music? Why? Tell your partner.

> My favorite kind of music is jazz. I like it because…

7 Listening   Class CD1 Track 39

A People are talking about music. What kind of music does each person talk about?
Listen and check (✓) the correct answer.

	Classical	Hip-hop	Jazz	Pop	Rock
1.	❑	❑	❑	❑	❑
2.	❑	❑	❑	❑	❑
3.	❑	❑	❑	❑	❑
4.	❑	❑	❑	❑	❑

B Listen again. Do the people like the music? Check (✓) *Yes* or *No*.

1. ❑ Yes   2. ❑ Yes   3. ❑ Yes   4. ❑ Yes
   ❑ No   ❑ No   ❑ No   ❑ No

8 Grammar: *Invitations and suggestions*

Class CD1
Track 40

A Listen. Then listen again and repeat.

Let's go to a rock concert next weekend.	**OK. That sounds like fun.**
How about listening to some blues tonight?	**I'm sorry, I can't.** I have to study.
What about seeing a play?	**That's a great idea.**
Why don't we go to a jazz club this Friday?	**I'd love to, but I can't.** I'm busy that night.

B *Pair work.* Take turns suggesting things to do this weekend. Answer using the ideas below or your own ideas.

have a picnic   drive somewhere   watch DVDs
go out to dinner   visit a museum   see a movie

Let's have a picnic this weekend.   **That's a great idea.**

9 Conversation

Class CD1
Track 41

A *Pair work.* Listen to the conversation. Then practice with a partner.

A: By the way, are you doing anything on Saturday night? How about going to that new jazz club?

B: I'd like to, but I can't. I'm going to a basketball game with my brother.

A: Well, how about going some other time?

B: Sure. Why don't we go on Friday night? I'm free then.

A: Friday night sounds fine. What time should we meet?

B: Let's get together at 8:00. We can get something to eat first.

A: That's a good idea.

B *Pair work.* Practice the conversation again. Use different days, times, and activities.

Extra

Change partners. Practice the conversation again with your new partner.

A Think of three things you are planning to do next week. Write a short note about each activity on the calendar and the time.

B *Class activity.* Invite classmates to do the activities with you. Classmates may say "No" because they are busy or not interested. Find a different classmate to say "Yes" to each activity.

A: *Nami, are you free on Monday night?*
B: *Yes, I am.*
A: *Let's go to a hip-hop club.*
B: *OK. That sounds like fun.*
A: *Jung, are you free on Tuesday afternoon?*
C: *No, I'm sorry. I'm busy.*
A: *Emi, are you free on Tuesday afternoon?*
D: *Yes, I'm free.*
A: *How about listening to some jazz?*
D: *I'm sorry, but I really don't like jazz.*

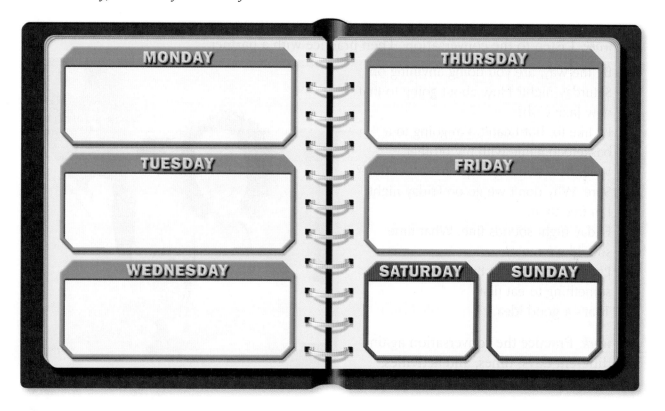

Extra

Tell a partner about your plans for the week.
On Monday night, I'm going to a hip-hop club with Nami. On Tuesday afternoon, I'm…

A city square

1. a post office
2. a library
3. an ATM
4. a coffee shop
5. a newsstand
6. a movie theater
7. a park
8. a hotel
9. a parking lot
10. a drugstore
11. a museum
12. a mailbox

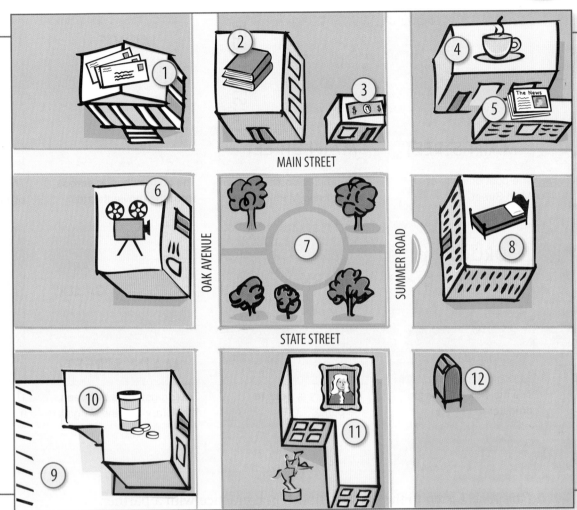

MAIN STREET

OAK AVENUE

SUMMER ROAD

STATE STREET

---

1 Speaking
Class CD1
Track 42

A Listen and look at the picture. Then practice with a partner.

A: What's this?
B: It's an ATM.

> **You can get money at an ATM.**

B What can you do at the places and things in the picture? Tell your partner.

2 Listening
Class CD1
Track 43

People are asking about places. Listen and number the places from 1 to 6.

___ drugstore	___ post office	___ newsstand
___ museum	___ hotel	___ park

Listen. Then listen again and repeat.

The post office is **on** Main Street.

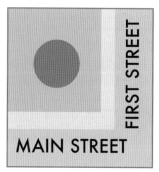

The hotel is **on the corner of** First and Main Streets.

The coffee shop is **across from** the movie theater.

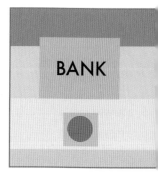

The newsstand is **in front of** the bank.

The mailbox is **near** the drugstore.

The library is **next to** the park.

The drugstore is **between** the library and the art gallery.

The parking lot is **behind** the museum.

4   **Conversation**
Class CD1
Track 45

A   *Pair work.* Listen to the conversation. Then practice with a partner.

> **A:** Excuse me. I think I'm lost. Is there a movie theater near here?
> **B:** Let me see. Oh, yes. There's one on Spring Street.
> **A:** Where on Spring Street?
> **B:** It's on the corner of Spring Street and Park Avenue.
> **A:** On the corner of Spring Street and Park Avenue?
> **B:** Yes. You can't miss it. It's across from the post office.
> **A:** Thank you!

B   *Pair work.* Take turns asking and answering questions about the places on the map on page 31.

Group work. Choose a place to "hide" on the map below. Partners ask Yes/No questions to find out exactly where you are hiding. Take turns.

A: *Are you on Elm Street?*
B: *No, I'm not.*
C: *Are you on Garden Street?*
B: *Yes, I am.*
C: *Are you near the mailbox?*
B: *No, I'm not.*
A: *Are you…?*

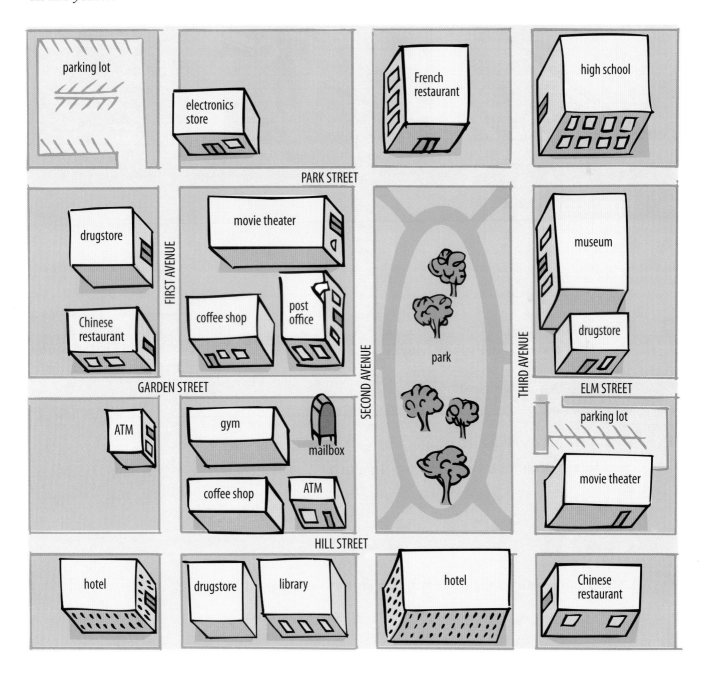

Public transportation

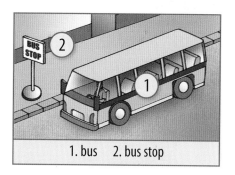
1. bus   2. bus stop

3. driver   4. passenger

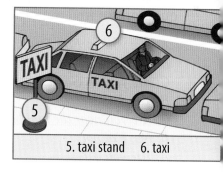
5. taxi stand   6. taxi

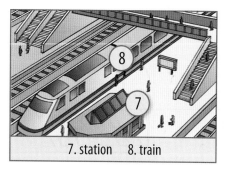
7. station   8. train

9. platform   10. conductor

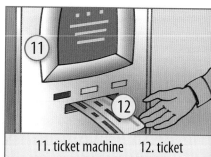
11. ticket machine   12. ticket

6 Speaking
Class CD1
Track 46

A Listen and look at the pictures. Then practice with a partner.

A: What's this?
B: It's a bus stop.

B What public transportation do you take? Where do you get on and off? Tell your partner.

> I take the bus. I get on at Main Street and First Avenue.

7 Listening
Class CD1
Track 47

A Where are the people? Listen and check (✓) the correct answer.

	In a station	On a bus	In a taxi	On a train
1.	❑	❑	❑	❑
2.	❑	❑	❑	❑
3.	❑	❑	❑	❑
4.	❑	❑	❑	❑

B Listen again. Match the people with the correct information.

1. The man ___   **a.** thinks the fare is inexpensive.
2. The woman ___   **b.** knows where the museum is.
3. The man ___   **c.** is going to Denver.
4. The woman ___   **d.** needs some change.

A Listen. Then listen again and repeat.

Wh- questions with *be*	Indirect questions
Where is the bus stop? **Where are** the ticket machines?	**Do you know where** the bus stop is? **Can you tell me where** the ticket machines are?

Wh- questions with *do*, *does*, or *did*	Indirect questions
How often do the trains leave? **What time** does the bank open? **How many** tickets did he buy?	**Do you know how often** the trains leave? **Can you tell me what time** the bank opens? **Do you know how many** tickets he bought?

Wh- questions with *can* or *should*	Indirect questions
Where can I get something to eat? **What** bus **should** we take?	**Could you tell me where** I **can** get something to eat? **Do you know what** bus we **should** take?

B *Pair work.* Make a *Wh-* question for your partner. Your partner changes it to an indirect question.

What time is it?   **Do you know what time it is?**

9 **Conversation** Class CD1
Track 49

A *Pair work.* Listen to the conversation. Then practice with a partner.

A: Excuse me. Could you tell me how often the buses to the city leave?

B: They leave every 15 minutes.

A: Can you tell me how long the bus ride is?

B: It takes about 45 minutes to get to the city center.

A: And do you know how much the fare is?

B: It's $12.00.

A: And just one more question. Could you tell me where I can buy a bus ticket?

B: There's a ticket machine next to the bus stop.

A: Oh, good. Thank you very much!

B *Pair work.* Practice the conversation again. Use information about public transportation in your city or town.

A Look at the questions in the chart. Change them to indirect questions.
Add two questions of your own.

B *Group work.* Use the questions to interview two classmates. Take notes about
their answers.

CITY SURVEY	Name ____	Name ____
1 What time do the banks open? *Do you know what time the banks open?* ___		
2 Where can I rent a cell phone? _____ ?		
3 Where is a good place to buy clothes? _____ ?		
4 What museums should people visit? _____ ?		
5 Where can I find a good hotel? _____ ?		
6 Where is a good place to meet friends? _____ ?		
7 Where can I get a good cup of coffee? _____ ?		
8 How much does a taxi to the airport cost? _____ ?		
9 _____ ?		
10 _____ ?		

C *Class activity.* Tell the class one or two interesting things you learned
about your city or town.

At a supermarket

1. juice
2. tofu
3. beef
4. chicken
5. carrots
6. tomatoes
7. milk
8. butter
9. eggs
10. cheese
11. fish
12. apples
13. oranges
14. bananas
15. potatoes
16. corn

1 Speaking

Class CD2
Track 2

A Listen and look at the pictures. Then practice with a partner.

A: What's this?
B: It's butter.

A: What are these?
B: They're eggs.

B Which foods and drinks do you have in your house right now? Which ones don't you have in your house? Tell your partner.

> I have some butter. I don't have (any) eggs. I have...

2 Listening

Class CD2
Track 3

People are talking about food. What are they going to eat? Listen and check (✓) the correct answers. There can be more than one answer for each item.

1. ❑ chicken   ❑ fish   ❑ carrots   ❑ potatoes
2. ❑ beef   ❑ corn   ❑ fish   ❑ eggs
3. ❑ yogurt   ❑ milk   ❑ bananas   ❑ apples
4. ❑ steak   ❑ tofu   ❑ corn   ❑ tomatoes

Listen. Then listen again and repeat.

Count nouns		Noncount nouns	
How many eggs are in the refrigerator?		**How much** milk is in the refrigerator?	
There are	**two or three.**	There is	**a little.**
	some.		**a lot.**
	a few.		**some.**
There are**n't**	**many.**	There is**n't**	**much.**
	any.		**any.**
There are	**none.**	There is	**none.**

Memo

not any = none

A *Pair work.* Listen to the conversation. Then practice with a partner.

A: I'm making a shopping list. What do we need?

B: Let's see. We need some tomatoes.

A: How many tomatoes should I get?

B: Not many. Get three or four. And we need some butter, too.

A: How much butter should I get?

B: A pound.

A: OK. Anything else?

B: No. That's all.

B *Pair work.* Practice the conversation again. Use different foods and drinks.

Group activity. Work in groups of three or four. Take turns.
Follow these instructions:

1. Choose a marker (an eraser, a coin, or a small piece of paper
   with your initials), and place it on START.

2. Toss a coin and move your marker one or two spaces. "Heads"
   means move one space. "Tails" means move two spaces.

3. Make a question for the answer in the space. Use *how much* or *how many*
   in the question. The other people in the group decide if the meaning and
   grammar of the answer are correct.

4. The first person to reach THE END is the winner.

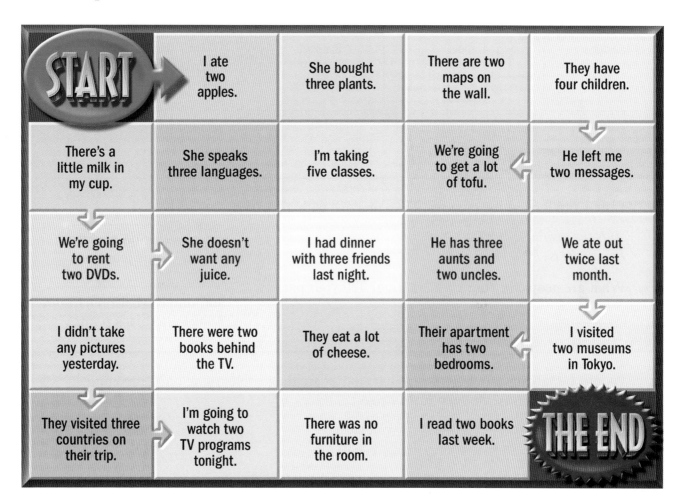

START →	I ate two apples.	She bought three plants.	There are two maps on the wall.	They have four children.
There's a little milk in my cup.	She speaks three languages.	I'm taking five classes.	We're going to get a lot of tofu.	He left me two messages.
We're going to rent two DVDs.	She doesn't want any juice.	I had dinner with three friends last night.	He has three aunts and two uncles.	We ate out twice last month.
I didn't take any pictures yesterday.	There were two books behind the TV.	They eat a lot of cheese.	Their apartment has two bedrooms.	I visited two museums in Tokyo.
They visited three countries on their trip.	I'm going to watch two TV programs tonight.	There was no furniture in the room.	I read two books last week.	THE END

Extra

Make up two answers about yourself for questions beginning with
how much or *how many*. Tell your answers to a partner. Your partner
makes questions for your answers.

A: *I have three watches.*

B: *How many watches do you have?*

Clothes and colors

1 a dress 2 a scarf 3 a jacket	4. shoes 5. a shirt 6. a tie 7. pants	8. a skirt 9. a coat 10. boots	11. a T-shirt 12. (blue) jeans 13. a cap	14. a sweater 15. socks 16. sneakers

6 Speaking
Class CD2
Track 6

A Listen and look at the pictures. Then practice with a partner.

A: Is she wearing a skirt?
B: Yes, she is. / No, she isn't.

> Hana is wearing a white shirt and blue jeans.

B What are people in your class wearing? Tell your partner.

> Sunjung is wearing a green T-shirt and black pants.

7 Listening
Class CD2
Track 7

A People are talking about clothes. What clothes are the people trying on? Listen and number the items of clothing from 1 to 6.

___ a T-shirt	___ a jacket	___ shoes
___ jeans	___ a skirt	___ boots

B Listen again. What's wrong with each item? Check (✓) the correct answer.

1. **a.** ❑ It's too short.
   b. ❑ It's too big.

2. **a.** ❑ They're too short.
   b. ❑ They're too long.

3. **a.** ❑ They're too big.
   b. ❑ They're too small.

4. **a.** ❑ They're too big.
   b. ❑ They're too small.

5. **a.** ❑ It's too long.
   b. ❑ It's too small.

6. **a.** ❑ It's too big.
   b. ❑ It's too short.

A Listen. Then listen again and repeat.

| Which dress do you **like better**, the blue one or the pink one? |
| I like the blue one **better** (**than** the pink one). |
| Which one is **cheaper / more stylish**? |
| The pink one is **cheaper / more stylish** (**than** the blue one). |
| Which shoes do you **like more**, yellow ones or green ones? |
| I like green ones **more** (**than** yellow ones). |

Memo

big → bigger
small → smaller
nice → nicer
pretty → prettier
expensive → more expensive
good → better
bad → worse

B *Pair work.* Talk about your preferences. Use the ideas below or your own ideas. Take turns.

jeans (blue / black)　　T-shirts (white / colorful)
clothes (expensive / inexpensive)

> **I like red boots more than brown ones. They're more stylish.**

Helpful Language
....
• The color is more attractive.
• The design is prettier.
• It's nicer.
• They're more stylish.

A *Pair work.* Listen to the conversation. Then practice with a partner.

A: So, which jacket are you going to buy? The black one or the red one?

B: Well, I like the black one a lot, but I also like the red one. I really can't decide which one I like better. What do you think?

A: I like the black one better. It's more stylish.

B: Well, it is more stylish, but it's also a lot more expensive.

A: Yeah, but it also looks better on you.

B: Do you really think so?

A: Yes, really. And the quality is better, too. I think you should buy the black one.

B: You're right. It's more attractive. I'm going to buy it.

B *Pair work.* Practice the conversation again using different items of clothing and different adjectives.

A *Group work.* Work in a group of three or four. Look at the adjectives in the box. Think of other adjectives you know and write them in the box.

Adjectives

pretty	_____	_____	_____
expensive	_____	_____	_____
big	_____	_____	_____
good	_____	_____	_____
nice	_____	_____	_____

B *Group work.* Choose two pictures. Make a sentence comparing the items in the pictures you choose. Use the adjectives in the box or other adjectives you know. Take turns.

A: *A bicycle is bigger than a chicken.*
B: *An airplane is more expensive than a sofa.*

Shops and stores

1. clothing store
2. bookstore
3. shoe store
4. jewelry store
5. sporting goods store
6. furniture store
7. music store
8. stationery store
9. video store
10. pet store
11. bakery
12. pizza place
13. hair salon
14. ice cream shop

1 Speaking

Class CD2
Track 10

A Listen and look at the picture. Then practice with a partner.

> A: Where's the shoe store?
> B: It's here.

B What can you get at the places in the picture? Tell your partner.

> You can get shoes and boots at a shoe store.

2 Listening

Class CD2
Track 11

What kind of store are the people shopping in? Listen and check (✓) the correct answer.

	Video store	Shoe store	Pizza place	Clothing store	Stationery store
1.	❏	❏	❏	❏	❏
2.	❏	❏	❏	❏	❏
3.	❏	❏	❏	❏	❏
4.	❏	❏	❏	❏	❏
5.	❏	❏	❏	❏	❏

Listen. Then listen again and repeat.

How do I get to the bookstore?
Go up Pine Street. **Go** one block. **Turn right** on Center Street. The bookstore is **on the left**.

Memo

You can also say:
Walk up / down Pine Street.
Drive up / down Oak Street.

How can I get to the music store?
Go down Oak Street. **Go** two blocks. **Turn left** on State Street. The music store is **on the right**.

Memo

← left
→ right

4 Conversation

Class CD2
Track 13

A *Pair work.* Listen to the conversation. Then practice with a partner.

A: Excuse me. How do we get to Rick's Ice Cream Shop?

B: Rick's Ice Cream Shop? Let's see. Go up this street. Walk one block. Turn right on West Street. Walk two more blocks. Rick's Ice Cream Shop is on the left.

A: OK. Go one block up this street. Turn right on West Street. Go two more blocks. Rick's Ice Cream Shop is on the left.

B: That's right. You can't miss it.

A: Thank you.

B *Pair work.* Practice the conversation again. Ask about places in your city and give true answers.

Extra

Draw a map of the neighborhood where you live. Include your home, the streets around it, stores, restaurants, and other important places. Then give your map to your partner. Your partner asks you how to get from one place on your map to another.

A: *How do I get from the bakery to the hair salon?*

B: *Go out of the bakery. Turn left. Go down the street two blocks...*

Student A looks at this page. Student B looks at page 73.

A *Pair work.* Look at the map. You and your partner are on Oak Street between Second and Third Avenues. Your partner asks for directions to four places. There are signs for the places in red on your map. Give your partner directions to the places.

> B: *Excuse me. I'm looking for a video store.*
> A: *A video store? Let's see. Go down…*

Helpful Language

- Go up / down…
  It's on the right / left. It's near…
- Walk up / down…
  It's on the corner of… It's next to…
- Go one block / two blocks.
  It's across from… It's behind…
- Turn right / left.
  It's in front of… It's between…

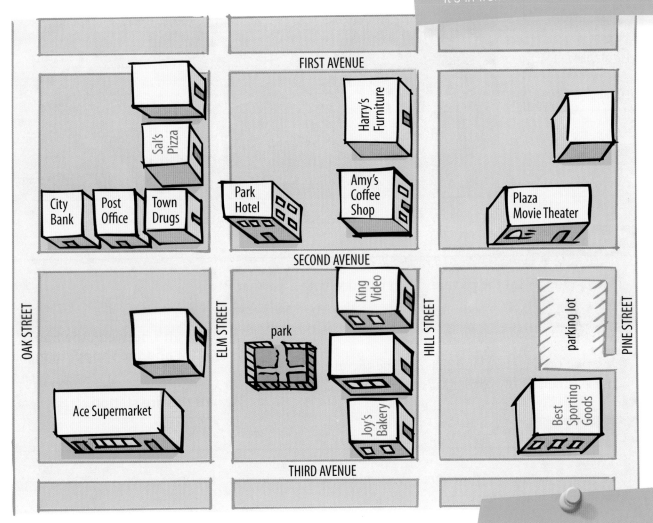

B *Pair work.* Look at the map. You and your partner are on Oak Street between Second and Third Avenues. Ask your partner for directions to these four places. Then write the places on your map.

a shoe store   a bookstore   an ice cream shop   a hair salon

> A: *Excuse me. I'm looking for a shoe store.*
> B: *A shoe store? Let's see. Go down…*

Helpful Language

- Do I turn right or left?
- Then what do I do?
- OK. I understand.

Places around town

1. police station
2. stadium
3. (shopping) mall
4. fire station
5. tunnel
6. bridge
7. river
8. bank
9. gas station
10. pond
11. city hall / town hall
12. hospital

---

6 Speaking
 Class CD2
Track 14

A Listen and look at the picture. Then practice with a partner.

A: Is this the bank?
B: No, it isn't. It's the stadium.

> It's between the bank and the shopping mall.

B Describe the location of a place in the picture to your partner. Your partner says the name of the place.

> It's the fire station.

---

7 Listening
 Class CD2
Track 15

A People are asking for directions. What places are they looking for? Listen and number the places from 1 to 4.

____ stadium   ____ gas station   ____ city hall   ____ police station

B Listen again. Check (✓) the correct directions.

1. **a.** ❑ Turn right at the bank.   **b.** ❑ Turn right after the bank.
2. **a.** ❑ Go two blocks up this street.   **b.** ❑ Go two blocks on this street.
3. **a.** ❑ Go right at the corner.   **b.** ❑ Turn right at the corner.
4. **a.** ❑ Walk along the block.   **b.** ❑ Walk one block.

A Listen. Then listen again and repeat.

Go **straight**.

Go **past** the bank.

Go **through** the tunnel.

Go **around** the pond.

Go **over** the bridge.

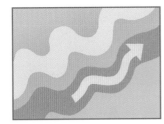
Go **along** the river.

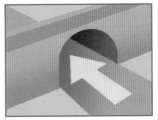
Go **under** the bridge.

Go **across** the street.

B *Pair work.* Look at the picture on page 46. Make sentences about where the people and things in the picture are going. Take turns.

> The boat is going under the bridge.

A *Pair work.* Listen to the conversation. Then practice with a partner.

A: Excuse me. I think I'm lost. Is there a police station near here?

B: Yes, there's a police station over on River Street.

A: How do I get to River Street?

B: Let's see. Go straight up this street. Go past the park. Then go over the bridge. Turn right after the bridge, and then go along the river. The police station is on the left.

A: Got it! Thanks a lot for your help.

B: Don't mention it.

B *Pair work.* Practice the conversation again. Ask for and give information about places in your city or town.

A Look at the map. You are at START. Think about how to give directions from START to different places on the map.

B *Group work.* Work in a group of three or four. Take turns. Give directions to a place on the map. Don't say the place. Then ask "Where are you now?" Group members say where they are.

A: *Walk up Park Avenue. Go past the pond. Turn right on Elm Street. Go over the bridge. Turn left and walk along the river. Go straight for one block. Turn right on First Street. Where are you now?*

B: *We are at…*

Helpful Language

• Then what do we do?
• Do we turn right or left?
• Did you say "First Street" or "Third Street"?
• Where do we turn?
• How many blocks do we go?

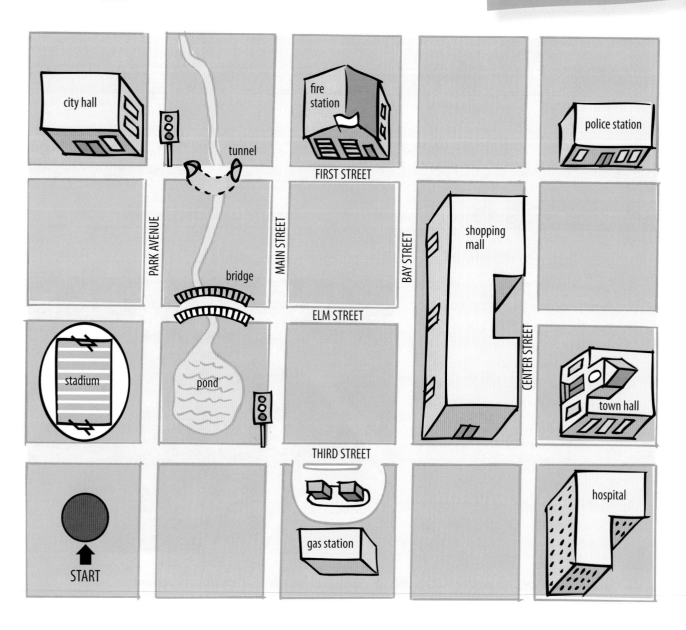

Hobbies

Things people collect

caps

stamps

comic books

trading cards

Things people play

chess

cards

board games

guitar

Other activities

surf the Internet

do puzzles

go snowboarding

paint

1 Speaking
 Class CD2
Track 18

A Listen and look at the pictures. Then practice with a partner.

> A: *What does he collect?*
> B: *He collects caps.*

B Which of these hobbies do you like? Tell your partner.

> **I like to collect comic books, and I like to play cards.**

2 Listening
 Class CD2
Track 19

People are talking about their hobbies. Listen and number the hobbies from 1 to 6.

___ painting   ___ collecting stamps   ___ playing board games
___ snowboarding   ___ playing chess   ___ collecting comic books

3 Grammar: *Verb + infinitive*

 Class CD2
Track 20

Listen. Then listen again and repeat.

I	like	to do	puzzles.	**Some other verbs followed by the infinitive**
	don't like	to play	video games.	**decide**
	love	to collect	comic books.	**learn** **plan**
	want	to go	snowboarding.	**would like**
	hate	to be	indoors.	

4 Conversation

 Class CD2
Track 21

A *Pair work.* Listen to the conversation. Then practice with a partner.

A: What do you like to do in your free time?
B: Me? I like to play cards. How about you?
A: Well, to be honest, I don't like to play cards very much. But I love to play chess.
B: Really? I like to play chess, too! Do you have any other hobbies?
A: Oh yeah, I like to collect things. I have a huge stamp collection.
B: No kidding. I'd like to see it sometime.
A: Well, why don't we get together tomorrow? I can show it to you then.
B: OK. Let's plan to meet at three o'clock.
A: Sounds good.

B *Pair work.* Practice the conversation again. Use different names, hobbies, and times.

> ### Extra
>
> Think of two or three things you collected, played, or did in your free time when you were younger. How old were you? What did you do? Tell your partner.
>
> *When I was ten years old, I played the piano. When I was twelve years old, I...*

A Look at the hobbies on the cards below. Which of these hobbies do you do?

B *Class activity.* Do people in your class have these hobbies? Find one classmate for each hobby. Write your classmates' names and any extra information.

> *A: Hiro, do you collect trading cards?*
> *B: Yes, I do.*
> *A: What kind of cards do you collect?*
> *B: I collect baseball cards.*

_____ collects trading cards. (Find out what kind of cards.)
_____

_____ plays chess. (Find out how well.)
_____

_____ does puzzles. (Find out what kind.)
_____

_____ surfs the Internet. (Find out how often.)
_____

_____ collects stamps. (Find out why.)
_____

_____ plays board games. (Find out what games.)
_____

_____ paints. (Find out when.)
_____

_____ collects coins. (Find out what kind.)
_____

_____ plays the guitar. (Find out what kind of music he or she plays.)
_____

_____ collects comic books. (Find out his or her favorite comic book.)
_____

_____ plays video games. (Find out what games.)
_____

_____ plays cards. (Find out who with.)
_____

C *Group work.* Tell your partners about your classmates' hobbies. Give as many details as you can. Take turns.

Hiro collects baseball cards. He has more than 200 cards.

Indoor exercise

do yoga

box

lift weights

play table tennis

do judo

wrestle

6 Speaking
Class CD2
Track 22

A Listen and look at the pictures. Then practice with a partner.

A: Are they doing yoga?
B: Yes, they are.

B What do you do for exercise? Tell your partner.

> I do yoga, and
> I play basketball.

7 Listening
Class CD2
Track 23

A People are talking about indoor sports and activities. Listen and number the sports and activities they like from 1 to 6.

___ judo   ___ wrestling   ___ weight lifting
___ yoga   ___ table tennis   ___ boxing

B Listen again. Check (✓) the best response.

1. **a.** ❑ I do judo.
    b. ❑ No, I don't.

2. **a.** ❑ That's interesting.
    b. ❑ Yes, I do.

3. **a.** ❑ Yeah, you're right.
    b. ❑ Yeah, it's my favorite sport.

4. **a.** ❑ No, thanks. I'm tired.
    b. ❑ Yeah, I'm crazy about it.

5. **a.** ❑ Yeah, I'm tired.
    b. ❑ Yeah, I love it.

6. **a.** ❑ At the health club.
    b. ❑ Yes. Before breakfast.

8 Grammar: *Verb + noun*

Class CD2
Track 24

A Listen. Then listen again and repeat.

I	enjoy	yoga.	Some other verbs or phrases followed by nouns
	love like don't like can't stand	boxing. judo. table tennis. wrestling.	**be interested in** **prefer** **dislike** **hate**

Memo
A noun or noun phrase can follow many different verbs.

B *Pair work.* How do you feel about these activities? Tell your partner.

singing   working   talking   studying
volleyball   soccer   tennis   golf

I can't stand singing.

9 Conversation

Class CD2
Track 25

A *Pair work.* Listen to the conversation. Then practice with a partner.

A: You're in good shape, Cara. How do you do it?

B: Well, I go the gym three times a week, and I do yoga for about two hours.

A: Two hours? That's a lot.

B: Yeah, it is, but I really enjoy yoga. What about you? What do you do to keep in shape?

A: Me? I was on the wrestling team when I was in high school, but I don't do it anymore. Now I'm into boxing.

B: Boxing? No kidding.

A: Yeah, I really like boxing.

B *Pair work.* Practice the conversation again. Use different sports or activities.

Extra

Continue the conversation in A. Find out at least three activities that you and your partner both enjoy. Ask:
Do you enjoy…?   Do you like…?   Are you interested in…?
If you agree, say:
Me, too!   So do I!   So am I!   I do, too!   I am, too!

Group activity. Work in groups of three or four. Take turns. Follow these instructions.

heads

tails

1. Choose a marker (an eraser, a coin, or a small piece of paper with your initials) and place it on **START**.

2. Toss a coin and move your marker one or two spaces. "Heads" means move one space. "Tails" means move two spaces.

3. Answer the question or do the task written in the space.

4. The first person to reach **THE END** is the winner.

Start

What are some popular board games?

Go ahead one space.

Talk for 20 seconds about your favorite hobby.

Toss again.

What school subjects are you most interested in?

What is one thing you hate to do?

What is something you did when you were little that you don't do now?

Lose a turn.

Do you collect anything? What?

Go back two spaces.

Where do you exercise?

Go ahead three spaces.

Talk for 20 seconds about a sport you like to watch.

Toss again.

Does anyone in your family like to paint? Who?

Can you play a musical instrument? Which one?

Go ahead one space.

What card games do you know how to play?

Talk for 20 seconds about a sport you like to play.

Lose a turn.

What is one thing you love to do in your free time?

Go back three spaces.

What is your favorite indoor sport?

What is your favorite outdoor sport?

What are some things you like to do on the weekend?

Go back one space.

Does anyone you know play the guitar?

What kind of exercise are you planning to do soon?

The End

Travel plans

go backpacking

go rafting

take a guided tour

take a bus tour

go skiing

go on a train trip

take a cruise

go to the beach

I **Speaking**   Class CD2
Track 26

A Listen and look at the pictures. Then practice with a partner.

A: What are their travel plans?
B: They're going backpacking.

> I think going rafting is the most exciting.

B Which travel plan do you think is the most exciting? the most relaxing? the cheapest? the most interesting? the most expensive? the safest? Tell your partner.

---

2 **Listening**   Class CD2
Track 27

A man is talking about his travel plans. What is he going to do? Listen and number the pictures from 1 to 5.

a.

b.

c.

d.

e.

3 Grammar: *Future plans with* be going to *and* will

Class CD2
Track 28

Listen. Then listen again and repeat.

What	**are** you **going to**	**do**?	I'**m going to go** backpacking. I'**m not going to go** on a guided tour.
Where	**are** you **going to**	**stay**?	I'm not sure. I think I'**ll go** camping. I probably **won't stay** in a hotel.

Memo

Use *be going to* + verb for plans that are definite.

Use *will* + verb for possible plans.

4 Conversation

Class CD2
Track 29

A   *Pair work.* Listen to the conversation. Then practice with a partner.

A: I'm so excited. I'm going to Canada for two weeks!

B: Wow! That *is* exciting. What are you going to do there? Are you going to take a guided tour?

A: No, I'm not. I'm going to go backpacking with some friends. And maybe we'll do some white-water rafting. What about you? Any travel plans?

B: Yeah. I'm going to go to Thailand.

A: Thailand? That's great! How long are you going to stay?

B: I'm not sure. I'll probably stay about a week.

B   *Pair work.* Practice the conversation again. Use different travel plans.

Helpful Language

• When did you go?
• Who did you go with?
• How long did you stay?
• Did you have a good time?

Extra

Talk about a recent trip. Say where you went and what kind of trip it was. Partners ask questions.

A: *Last year I went on a trip to Hakuba. It was a ski trip.*

B: *How long did you stay?*

A: *(I stayed) five days.*

56   Unit 10

Student A looks at this page. Student B looks at page 74.

A *Pair work.* Look at the travel brochure. You are going to take the Australian surfing trip in the brochure. Your partner is going on a different trip. Find out as much as you can about your partner's trip. Use these and your own ideas to ask questions.

- what kind of trip he or she is going to take
- how long he or she is going to stay
- what places he or she is going to visit
- where he or she is going to stay
- what he or she is going to do
- what he or she thinks will be most fun

A: So, what kind of trip are you going to take?

B: I'm going to take…

A: How long are you going to stay?

B: I'm going to stay…

Australian Surfing Tour

15-day tour
We'll take you to unforgettable Australian surfing destinations such as:

- Kira • Margaret River • Shark Island
- Black Rock • Bells

Surfboard rental and daily surfing classes are included in the low price! You'll enjoy a welcoming stay at beachfront hotels with fine restaurants.

Evening Activities
- Beach Barbecues
- Dinner Cruises
- Dancing

Other Sports
- Swimming
- Sailing
- Beach Volleyball
- Windsurfing

B *Pair work.* Answer your partner's questions about your trip. Use your imagination to answer questions you don't have definite answers for.

B: How long are you going to stay in each place?

A: I'm not sure. I'll probably stay two or three days in each place.

Trip preparations

apply for a visa

book a flight

reserve a hotel room

buy a guidebook

change some money

pack

6 Speaking
Class CD2
Track 30

A Listen and look at the pictures. Then practice with a partner.

A: Is she applying for a visa?
B: Yes, she is.

> **Memo**
> Book a flight / room and reserve a flight / room have the same meaning.

B Imagine you are going to another country.
What do you need to do before you go? Tell your partner.

> I'm going to England. I need to get a visa and...

7 Listening
Class CD2
Track 31

A People are talking about trips they will be taking. What do they need to do? Listen and circle the correct answer.

1. **a.** pack   **b.** apply for a visa   **c.** buy a guidebook
2. **a.** change some money   **b.** book a flight   **c.** apply for a visa
3. **a.** book a flight   **b.** change some money   **c.** apply for a visa
4. **a.** reserve a hotel room   **b.** buy some clothes   **c.** pack

B Listen again. Match the people and the information. Write the correct letter.

1. She ___   **a.** is leaving tomorrow.
2. He ___   **b.** didn't have time to do it last week.
3. She ___   **c.** used the Internet to do something.
4. He ___   **d.** wants to buy a new one.

A   Listen. Then listen again and repeat.

Where do you usually **like to** go on vacation?
 I **like to** go to Vietnam. My favorite place is China Beach.
Do you **like to** go swimming when you're in Vietnam?
 Yes, I **do**. / No, I **don't**.

Where **would** you **like to** go on your next vacation?
 I'**d like to** go to Switzerland.
Would you **like to** go skiing in Switzerland?
 Yes, I **would**. / No, I **wouldn't**.

Memo

I **like** to go = I enjoy going
I'**d like** to go = I want to go

B   *Pair work.* Ask and answer questions with your partner. Use different places and activities.

Where do you like
to go on vacation?

I like to go to Tahiti. My
favorite place is Point Venus.

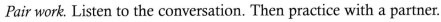

9 **Conversation**   Class CD2
Track 33

A   *Pair work.* Listen to the conversation. Then practice with a partner.

A: Do you like to travel, Jo-eun?
B: Sure! I love to travel, but I don't like to travel by car or bus.
A: Why not?
B: I get sick in cars and buses. I like to go by train or plane whenever I can.
A: Would you like to take a trip around the world someday?
B: Of course I would.
A: Would you like to go by plane?
B: No, I wouldn't. But, I'd like to go on a cruise around the world. I think that would be a lot of fun.
A: I think so, too.

B   *Pair work.* Practice the conversation again using different travel ideas.

Extra

What do you and your partner like to do when you travel? Find two things you both like to do. Find two things you don't like to do. Use the ideas below or your own ideas.
A: *I like to stay in hotels when I travel.*
B: *Me, too. / I don't.*

meet new people	stay in hotels	take guided tours
try new foods	use credit cards	take photos
go sightseeing	rent a car	buy souvenirs

A   Think about a trip you would like to take. Look at the questions. Make notes below to answer the questions.

What kind of trip would you like to take?

_____

_____

Where would you like to go?

_____

_____

_____

_____

_____

When would you like to go?

_____

_____

_____

How long would you like to stay?

_____

_____

_____

_____

_____

What would you like to do?

_____

_____

_____

_____

_____

What would you like to see?

_____

_____

_____

_____

_____

Who would you like to go with?

_____

_____

_____

What kinds of food would you like to eat?

_____

_____

_____

B   *Group work.* Tell the group about your trip. Answer your partners' questions. Take turns.

I would like to take a vacation at a beach. I'd like to go to…

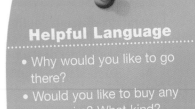

Helpful Language

- Why would you like to go there?
- Would you like to buy any souvenirs? What kind?
- Would you take any photos?

Extra

As a group, decide on a vacation that everyone would like to take together.

Quantities

a bag

a bottle

a box

a can

a slice

a cup

a glass

a spoonful

a plate

a bowl

a carton

a container

a jar

a six-pack

a loaf

---

1 Speaking   Class CD2 Track 34

A Listen and look at the pictures. Then practice with a partner.

> *A: What's this?*
> *B: It's a bag of rice.*

B What quantities of foods and drinks do you have at home? Tell your partner.

> I have a bottle of soda at home. I also have...

---

2 Listening   Class CD2 Track 35

People are talking about foods and drinks. What quantities do they mention?
Listen and circle the correct answer.

1. a <u>carton / bottle</u> of milk

2. a <u>can / glass</u> of tomato juice

3. a <u>bottle / jar</u> of soda

4. a <u>box / plate</u> of spaghetti

5. a <u>loaf / slice</u> of bread

6. a <u>cup / can</u> of coffee

3 Grammar: A ... of ...

Class CD2
Track 36

Listen. Then listen again and repeat.

	bag		potato chips
	bottle		water
a	box	of	popcorn
	bowl		rice
	can		beans

	cup		tea
	glass		juice
a	piece	of	pie
	slice		bread
	spoonful		sugar

4 Conversation

Class CD2
Track 37

A *Pair work.* Listen to the conversation. Then practice with a partner.

A: I'm going to have a glass of iced tea. What about you?

B: I'd like a cup of coffee.

A: What are you going to have to eat?

B: I'm not sure. Everything looks so delicious! Maybe I'll get the chocolate cream pie. What about you?

A: Hmm... I think I'll have a piece of that carrot cake.

B: Oh, you'll like that. The carrot cake here is excellent!

A: Good. Listen, why don't you go and sit down at a table? I'll order everything. Let me think... That'll be one glass of iced tea, one cup of coffee, a slice of chocolate cream pie, and a piece of carrot cake. Right?

B: That's right.

B *Pair work.* Practice the conversation again. Use different foods and drinks.

Extra

What things can you buy in these containers? Work in a small group and name three things for each container.

bag	bottle	box	can	carton
_____	_____	_____	_____	_____
_____	_____	_____	_____	_____
_____	_____	_____	_____	_____

Student A looks at this page. Student B looks at page 75.

A   Look at the picture. What foods and drinks can you see? In what quantities?
Make notes.

There is a carton of… There are two containers of…

B   *Pair work.* Your picture and Student B's picture are not the same.
Find out what is different. Ask about foods, drinks, and quantities.

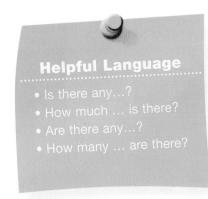

Helpful Language

- Is there any…?
- How much … is there?
- Are there any…?
- How many … are there?

Extra

Look at Student B's picture on page 75 for 30 seconds. Then close
your book. Can you remember what quantities of foods and drinks
are in the picture? Say as much as you can about Student B's
picture.

Cooking

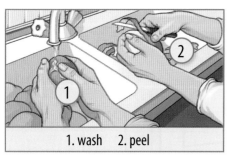

1. wash   2. peel

3. boil   4. stir

5. chop   6. slice

7. pour   8. add

9. put in   10. turn on

11. bake   12. fry

6 Speaking

Class CD2
Track 38

A Listen and look at the pictures. Then practice with a partner.

A: What's she doing?
B: She's peeling potatoes.

B Which of these things can you do? Tell your partner.

I can fry fish. I can...

7 Listening

Class CD2
Track 39

A A woman is giving directions for making Easy Baked Spaghetti. Listen and number the steps from 1 to 5.

a.

b.

c.

d.

e.

B Listen again. Number the verbs 1 to 5 in the order you hear them.

___ add   ___ bake   ___ pour   ___ put in   ___ stir

A Listen. Then listen again and repeat.

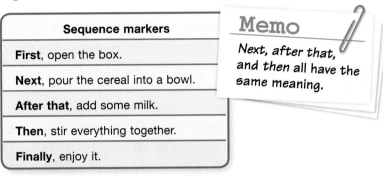

Imperatives
Add a little salt.
Don't add water.
Fry the onions.
Don't fry the potatoes.

Sequence markers
First, open the box.
Next, pour the cereal into a bowl.
After that, add some milk.
Then, stir everything together.
Finally, enjoy it.

Memo
Next, after that, and then all have the same meaning.

B *Pair work*. Number these instructions in the correct order. Then say them using sequence markers.

OK, first, ...

___ take the soda
___ put the coins into the machine

___ push the button
___ take out some coins

___ drink it

9 **Conversation** Class CD2 Track 41

A *Pair work*. Listen to the conversation. Then practice with a partner.

A: Excuse me. Can you show me how to use this microwave?

B: Sure. First, you need to open the door of the oven and put your dish inside.

A: OK. Then what?

B: Next, choose the cooking time.

A: And what do I do after that?

B: Then, close the door.

A: Uh-huh. Then, what do I do?

B: Finally, touch *Start* to turn the oven on.

A: Oh, I see! Thanks a lot.

B *Pair work*. Practice the conversation again. Use the appliances below or other machines you know.

coffeemaker
electric can opener

rice cooker
electric hot pot

Extra

First, write a recipe (instructions for how to cook something) or instructions for doing something else. Then, read your instructions to your partner. Make sure your partner understands completely, and answer any questions he or she has.

Student A looks at this page. Student B looks at page 76.

A *Pair work.* The pictures below show a recipe for carrot rounds. The pictures are not in order. Find out the correct order from your partner. Ask your partner how to make carrot rounds. Number the pictures from 1 to 6.

Carrot Rounds

A: How do you make carrot rounds?
B: Well, first, …
A: OK. Then what?
B: Then, …
A: And what's the next step?

B *Pair work.* Your partner asks you how to make an orange banana smoothie. Use the recipe below to give directions.

Orange Banana Smoothie
1. Peel 1 banana.
2. Slice the banana.
3. Put the banana in a blender.
4. Pour 1 cup of orange juice into the blender.
5. Add 3 spoonfuls of yogurt.
6. Turn on the blender.

Helpful Language
• Do you understand?
• Should I repeat that?
• Should I continue?

Extra

Look at the pictures in **A** above. Explain each step of the recipe for carrot rounds to your partner. Your partner corrects any mistakes you make.

Job skills

build houses

cook

drive a truck

use a computer

sell

teach

Buenos días!
speak another language

interview people

write business letters

take care of children

repair computers

design web pages

1 Speaking
Class CD2
Track 42

A Listen and look at the pictures. Then practice with a partner.

A: *What can he do?*
B: *He can build houses.*

I can't build houses.
I can cook. I…

B Which of these things can you do? Which ones can't you do? Tell your partner.

2 Listening
Class CD2
Track 43

People are talking about their skills. What can they do? Listen and write *Sumi*,
Clive, Alice, Wang, Sissy, or *Niran* beside each skill.

1. _____ can cook French food.
2. _____ can repair computers.
3. _____ can speak Chinese.

4. _____ can design web pages.
5. _____ can speak Korean.
6. _____ can use a computer.

Class CD2
Track 44

Listen. Then listen again and repeat.

Can	Know how to
I **can drive** a car. I **can't drive** a truck. He **can build** houses. He **can't build** boats.	I **know how to repair** computers. I **don't know how to repair** TVs. She **knows how to speak** Japanese. She **doesn't know how to speak** Chinese.

Can you **cook**?
  Yes, I **can**. / No, I **can't**.
	Do you **know how to design** web pages?
	  Yes, I **do**. / No, I **don't**.

Can she **interview** people?
  Yes, she **can**. / No, she **can't**.
	Does he **know how to write** business letters?
	  Yes, he **does**. / No, he **doesn't**.

What **can** you **do**?
  I **can speak** Spanish.
	What **do** you **know how to do**?
	  I **know how to use** a computer.

4   **Conversation**   Class CD2
Track 45

A   *Pair work.* Listen to the conversation. Then practice with a partner.

    A: Do you know how to speak Spanish, Lisa?

    B: No, I don't. What about you? Can you speak Spanish?

    A: No, I can't, but Akira can. He knows how to speak Japanese, English, and Spanish.

    B: Wow! That's pretty good. How well can he speak Spanish?

    A: Very well. He learned it in Mexico.

    B: In Mexico? When was he in Mexico?

    A: He lived there when he was a kid.

    B: No kidding. I didn't know that.

B   *Pair work.* Practice the conversation again. Use different skills (cooking, repairing things, driving, building things, etc.).

Extra

Choose one of the topics below. Talk as long as you can about it. When you finish, your partner asks two questions.

- ▪ Talk about something you can repair.
- ▪ Talk about a dish you can cook.
- ▪ Talk about a machine you can use.

Communication task: Skills survey

A Look at the survey forms below. Add one question to each form.

B *Class activity.* Interview three classmates. Use a different form for each classmate. Ask follow-up questions after each Yes/No question. Write answers to follow-up questions in the *More information* columns.

Sample follow-up questions

How well can you...?   *When / Where did you learn how to...?*

Would you like to know how to...?   *Do you like to...?*

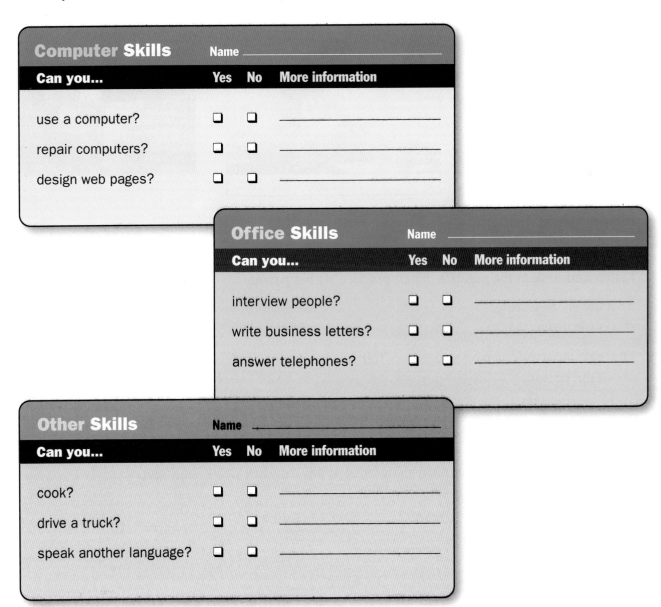

Computer Skills Name _____

Can you...	Yes	No	More information
use a computer?	❏	❏	_____
repair computers?	❏	❏	_____
design web pages?	❏	❏	_____

Office Skills Name _____

Can you...	Yes	No	More information
interview people?	❏	❏	_____
write business letters?	❏	❏	_____
answer telephones?	❏	❏	_____

Other Skills Name _____

Can you...	Yes	No	More information
cook?	❏	❏	_____
drive a truck?	❏	❏	_____
speak another language?	❏	❏	_____

C *Group work.* Work in groups of four or five students. Compare your survey results. Make sentences about classmates with the same skills.

Both Kenji and Dai can cook spaghetti.

Artistic talents

act

dance

direct movies

draw

write music

sing

6 Speaking
Class CD2
Track 46

A Listen and look at the pictures. Then practice with a partner.

A: What are they doing?
B: They're acting.

B Describe an artistic person you know. Tell your partner about the person.

> My cousin Sook is very artistic. She can act, sing, and dance.

7 Listening
Class CD2
Track 47

A People are talking about their artistic talents. What can they do? Listen and number the talents from 1 to 4.

___ painting   ___ singing   ___ acting   ___ dancing

B Listen again. Check (✓) the correct answer.

1. Richard _____.
   a. ❑ works as a teacher
   b. ❑ makes a lot of money

2. Cleo _____.
   a. ❑ works with children
   b. ❑ is busy with her children

3. Joyce _____.
   a. ❑ only likes jazz
   b. ❑ likes all kinds of music

4. Takeshi _____.
   a. ❑ works in a theater
   b. ❑ works on TV

A Listen. Then listen again and repeat.

I **could sing** when I was a child.	How well **could** you **paint**?
He **could play** the piano at the age of five.	How well **could** she **act**?
Could you **draw** when you were a child? Yes, I **could**. / No, I **couldn't**.	
Could Alice **dance** when she was six? Yes, she **could**. / No, she **couldn't**.	

Memo
You can also use knew how to to talk about ability in the past.

B *Pair work.* Tell your partner about your abilities when you were a child. Use *I could* or *I knew how to*. Ask each other follow-up questions.

> I could ice-skate when I was a boy.

> How well could you ice-skate?

9 **Conversation** Class CD2
Track 49

A *Pair work.* Listen to the conversation. Then practice with a partner.

A: Hi, Cara. What are you doing?
B: I'm reading a book about Mozart.
A: Oh, Mozart! I love his music. What does the book say?
B: Well, this part is interesting. It says, "Mozart could play the piano when he was four. He could write music when he was five, but he couldn't write words."
A: That's interesting. By the way, what could you do when you were four? Could you write?
B: No, I couldn't. I could read, but I didn't know how to write.
A: How well could you read?
B: Not very well. I knew how to read a few words.

The Life of Mozart

B *Pair work.* Practice the conversation again. Use your imagination to talk about different skills and talents.

Helpful Language
When you agree:
• So could I.
• Me, too!
• I could, too.

 Extra
Continue the conversation. Find at least three things that you and your partner could do before the age of five.

A Look at the questions. Which ones would you like to answer? Think about how to answer them. Add three more questions of your own. Use *can, can't, could,* or *couldn't* in your questions.

Can you play a musical instrument?

_____ _____?

What is something your parents can do, but you can't?

Can you speak another language?

Name two sports you can play.

Name two board games you can play.

What is one thing you could do very well when you were ten?

What are two things you could do when you were one year old?

What are two things you couldn't do when you were five years old?

What is one thing you can do really well?

What is one thing you can't do very well?

What is something your grandparents couldn't do, but you can?

What couldn't you do in the past, but you can do now?

What could you do at the age of twelve that you couldn't do at the age of two?

What could you do as a baby, but you can't do now?

_____ _____?

What is something you can do, but your parents can't?

_____ _____?

B *Group work.* Point to a question and answer it. Partners ask for more information. Take turns.

A: (Pointing to question "Can you play a musical instrument?")
  Yes, I can.
B: *What instrument can you play?*
A: *I can play the piano.*
C: *What kind of music can you play?*
A: *I can play classical music and jazz.*

Student B looks at this page. Student A looks at page 45.

A *Pair work.* Look at the map. You and your partner are on Oak Street between Second and Third Avenues. Ask your partner for directions to these four places. Then write the places on your map.

a video store   a bakery   a pizza shop   a sporting goods store

> B: Excuse me. I'm looking for a video store.
> A: A video store? Let's see. Go down...

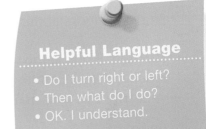

Helpful Language
- Do I turn right or left?
- Then what do I do?
- OK. I understand.

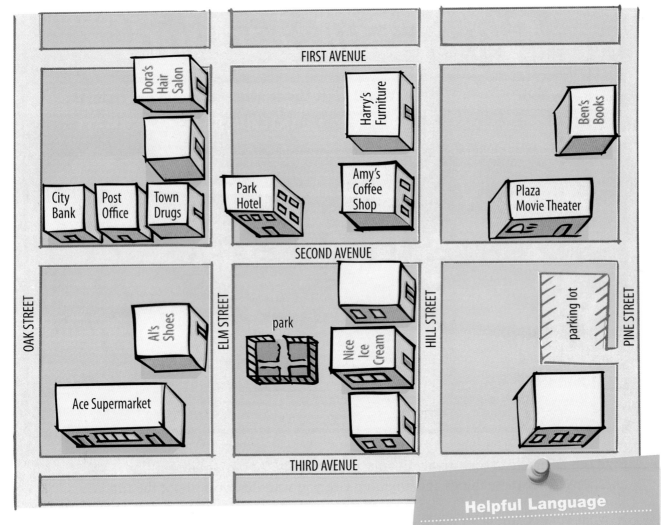

B *Pair work.* Look at the map. You and your partner are on Oak Street between Second and Third Avenues. Your partner asks for directions to four places. There are signs for the places in red on your map. Give your partner directions to the places.

> A: Excuse me. I'm looking for a shoe store.
> B: A shoe store? Let's see. Go down...

Helpful Language
- Go up / down...
  It's on the right / left. It's near...
- Walk up / down...
  It's on the corner of... It's next to...
- Go one block / two blocks.
  It's across from... It's behind...
- Turn right / left.
  It's in front of... It's between...

Student B looks at this page. Student A looks at page 57.

A *Pair work.* Look at the travel brochure. You are going to take the European ski trip in the brochure. Your partner is going on a different trip. Answer your partner's questions about your trip. Use your imagination to answer questions you don't have definite answers for.

A: How long are you going to stay in each place?
B: I'm not sure. I'll probably stay two or three days in each place.

Ski in Switzerland!

8-day tour **You'll visit these world-famous ski resorts:**

DAVOS • INTERLAKEN • ZERMATT

Ski equipment and daily ski lessons are included in the low price!
You'll enjoy a unique stay at charming mountainside hotels.

Evening Activities
• dancing
• deluxe restaurants
• classical music concerts
• karaoke clubs

Other Sports
• ice-skating
• snowboarding
• cross-country skiing

B Find out as much as you can about your partner's trip. Ask your partner questions about these things and anything else you want to know about the trip.

- what kind of trip he or she is going to take
- how long he or she is going to stay
- what places he or she is going to visit

- where he or she is going to stay
- what he or she is going to do
- what he or she thinks will be most fun

B: So, what kind of trip are you going to take?
A: I'm going to take…
B: How long are you going to stay?
A: I'm going to stay…

Student B looks at this page. Student A looks at page 63.

A   Look at the picture. What foods and drinks can you see? In what quantities?
Make notes.

There is a carton of… There are two containers of…

B   *Pair work.* Your picture and Student A's picture are not the
same. Find out what is different. Ask about foods, drinks, and
quantities.

Helpful Language

- Is there any…?
- How much … is there?
- Are there any…?
- How many … are there?

Extra

Look at Student A's picture on page 63 for 30 seconds. Then close
your book. Can you remember what quantities of foods and drinks
are in the picture? Say as much as you can about Student A's
picture.

Student B looks at this page. Student A looks at page 66.

A   *Pair work.* Your partner asks you how to make carrot rounds. Use the recipe below to give directions.

Carrot Rounds

1. Wash 2 carrots.
2. Slice the carrots.
3. Put the carrots in a pan.
4. Add 1 spoonful of butter and 1 spoonful of brown sugar.
5. Pour a little water into the pan.
6. Stir and cook for 5 minutes.

Helpful Language

- Do you understand?
- Should I repeat that?
- Should I continue?

A: *How do you make carrot rounds?*
B: *Well, first, …*
A: *OK. Then what?*
B: *Then, …*
A: *And what's the next step?*

B   *Pair work.* The pictures below show a recipe for an orange banana smoothie. The pictures are not in order. Find out the correct order from your partner. Ask your partner how to make an orange banana smoothie. Number the pictures from 1 to 6.

Orange Banana Smoothie

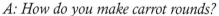

Extra

Look at the pictures in **B** above. Explain each step of the recipe for an orange banana smoothie to your partner. Your partner corrects any mistakes you make.

Check your English _____

Unit 1

A Vocabulary

Match the jobs with their descriptions.

accountant   actor   architect   chef   musician
salesperson   pilot   teacher   tour guide   web designer

1. This person cooks and prepares food. _chef_

2. This person's job is to show a place to tourists. _____

3. This person performs in a play or movie. _____

4. This person designs buildings. _____

5. This person plays a musical instrument. _____

6. This person flies an airplane. _____

7. This person's job is to sell things. _____

8. This person's job is to teach. _____

9. This person's job is to write or check financial records. _____

10. This person designs web pages. _____

B Grammar

Complete the questions.

1. **A:** How ____old are you____?   **B:** I'm 19 years old.

2. **A:** _____ from?   **B:** He's from New York.

3. **A:** _____ in Seoul?   **B:** No, I don't. I live in Pusan.

4. **A:** What company _____?   **B:** She works for MegaBank.

5. **A:** _____ to City University?   **B:** Yes, they do.

6. **A:** _____ hobbies?   **B:** I like to surf the Internet.

7. **A:** _____ a pilot?   **B:** Yes, I am.

8. **A:** _____ the subway?   **B:** No, I don't. I take the bus.

Check your English _____

Unit 2

A Vocabulary

Complete the sentences. Use the words below.

bored	angry	surprised	taking	working
excited	traveling	visiting	writing	studying

1. I can't sleep because I am so __excited__ about the trip.

2. I'm _____ Chinese because I have a test this afternoon.

3. Amy is _____ at Sam because he didn't invite her to the party.

4. My parents are on vacation in Europe. They're _____ in France.

5. She lives in Tokyo, but she is _____ friends in Sapporo right now.

6. I didn't know you were in Osaka. I was _____ to see you there.

7. Are you still _____ classes in English?

8. This TV program isn't very interesting. I'm _____ .

9. Cui is _____ in a restaurant to make some money.

10. I'm _____ a five-page paper for my history class.

B Grammar

Read the sentences. Correct the mistakes. There is one mistake in each pair of sentences.

1. I can't play tennis with ~~she~~ today. I'm going swimming with you.
    her

2. Seiji and me are going to see a movie today. Would you like to go with us?

3. My parents live in Pusan. I call they every Monday.

4. That tall man is looking at we. Do you know him?

5. Mr. Walker is my English teacher. I like he very much.

6. I'm talking to you. Please listen to I.

7. Jin-song loves Mei. Mei doesn't love he.

Check your English

Unit 3

A Vocabulary

Read the sentences. Complete the words.

1. Albert Einstein was an important s c i e n t i s t .

2. The book was really very interesting. In fact, it was f _ s _ i _ a _ i _ g .

3. What is the name of the _ r _ i _ t who painted these pictures?

4. The streets were c _ o _ d _ d with people.

5. The president is the _ e _ d _ r of our country.

6. Who is the d _ r _ c _ o _ of this movie?

7. This place is too n _ i _ _ for me. I like quiet places.

8. We visited many _ i _ t _ r _ c buildings in Paris.

9. Kuala Lumpur is a _ o _ _ _ n city.

10. Elizabeth I was a q _ e _ n of England.

B Grammar

Complete the questions.

1. A: _____ they in Guam? B: They were there a year ago.

2. A: _____ you born? B: I was born in Korea.

3. A: _____ he born in? B: He was born in Taipei.

4. A: _____ his occupation? B: He was an inventor.

5. A: _____ Yoko Ono's husband? B: His name was John Lennon.

6. A: _____ in England? B: I was there for two years.

7. A: _____ the weather? B: It was wonderful.

8. A: _____ with you? B: My father was with me.

9. A: _____ born in Spain? B: Yes, he was.

10. A: _____ happy in Europe? B: No, he wasn't. He was sad.

Check your English _____

Unit 4

A   Vocabulary

Complete the sentences. Use the words and phrases below.

get up   go sightseeing   nap   drive
barbecue   karaoke club   visit   watch

1. **A:** Did you _____ in Paris?

    B: Yes, I have pictures of all the places I visited.

2. Do you like to _____ museums?

3. Does Leda usually _____ early in the morning?

4. Mark likes to take a short _____ after lunch.

5. Who cooked the food at the _____?

6. **A:** Did you sing when you went to the _____?

    B: Oh, yes. Everyone did. They played really good songs at that place.

7. Did Mia _____ to work, or did she take the bus?

8. How many DVDs did you _____ last night?

B   Grammar

Complete the conversation. Use the simple past tense of the verbs in parentheses.

A: What __did__ (do) you and Junko do last night?

B: We _____ (get) together with some friends and _____ (have)
some pizza.

A: Where _____ (go) for pizza?

B: Oh, we _____ (not, go) out for pizza. We _____ (order) one
from Pizza King. What about you? _____ (do) you do anything interesting
last night?

A: Me? I _____ (not, do) very much. I _____ (read) a little.
Then I _____ (watch) an old horror movie on TV.

Check your English

A   Vocabulary

Complete the sentences. Use the words below.

classical	hip-hop	picnic	tournament
cafe	zoo	museum	country and western

1. People take food and eat it outdoors at a _____.

2. A _____ is a place with many different kinds of animals.

3. _____ is a type of dance music with a strong beat and spoken words.

4. A _____ is a building where you can see important pieces of art.

5. Mozart, Beethoven, and Bach all wrote _____ music.

6. A _____ is a small restaurant where people often get coffee or tea.

7. _____ is a style of music from the southern and western U.S.

8. Many golfers compete in a golf _____.

B   Grammar

Make a sentence with a similar meaning. Use the words in parentheses.

1. Let's go to a play tonight.   (play, to, how, tonight, about, a, going)

   _How about going to a play tonight?_____

2. What are they doing on Sunday?   (are, on, what, they, to, going, Sunday, do)

   _____

3. What about having a picnic?   (have, don't, we, why, picnic, a)

   _____

4. Why don't we see an opera tonight?   (about, what, opera, tonight, seeing, an)

   _____

5. He is not seeing a play.   (not, is, he, play, to, a, see, going)

   _____

6. When are we going to see a soccer match?   (match, seeing, when, we, a, are, soccer)

   _____

Check your English

Unit 6

A Vocabulary

Complete the crossword using the clues.

Across

2. You can read books at a _____.

3. The train stopped at the _____.

8. You need a _____ to ride a train.

10. How many _____ were on the train?

Down

1. We saw many beautiful paintings in the _____.

2. Park your car in the parking _____.

4. I bought this magazine at a _____.

5. We went for a walk in the _____.

6. You wait for a bus at a bus _____.

7. How much is the bus _____?

9. I sent a letter at the _____ office.

B Grammar

Put the words in order to make questions.

1. ticket / costs / know / do / you / much / a / how

   _____?

2. the / what / can / arrives / you / me / bus / time / tell

   _____?

3. tell / how / leave / you / me / often / trains / the / could / please

   _____?

4. can / I / where / know / taxi / you / get / do / a

   _____?

Check your English _____

Unit 7

A Vocabulary

Read the sentences. Complete the words.

1. You wear it on your head. It's a _c_ _ _.

2. You wear them on your feet. They're _ _ _ _k_ _.

3. It's a kind of meat. It's _ _ _ _f_.

4. They come from chickens. They're _ _ _g_ _.

5. It's a long orange vegetable. It's a _ _ _r_ _ _ _.

6. It's a drink. You can make it from oranges or apples. It's _j_ _ _ _c_ _.

7. You wear them on your feet to run. They're _ _n_ _ _ _ _ _r_ _.

8. You wear this around your neck or on your head. It's a _ _ _a_ _f_.

9. It's a red fruit. It's an _ _ _p_ _e_.

10. A man wears this around his neck with a shirt and jacket. It's a _ _i_ _.

B Grammar

Complete the conversation. Use the words and phrases below.

a little	a lot	how many	how much
like better	more	much	some

A: Which fruit do you _____, apples or oranges?

B: I like apples _____ than oranges.

A: Really? _____ apples do you eat?

B: I eat one apple every day, but I eat _____ of oranges, too.
What about you? _____ fruit do you eat?

A: I eat _____. I eat one or two bananas a week.

B: Gee, that isn't very _____.

A: I know. There are _____ of apples in my refrigerator. Do you want one?

Check your English

Unit 8

A Vocabulary

Complete the sentences. Use the words and phrases below.

furniture store	hospital	sporting goods store
bakery	shopping mall	stationery store

1. A _____ is a very large building with a lot of stores in it.

2. You can buy tables and chairs at a _____.

3. You can see sick people and doctors at a _____.

4. You can buy a baseball or a basketball at a _____.

5. People buy cakes and cookies at a _____.

6. You can buy pens, pencils, and paper at a _____.

B Grammar

Read the sentences and follow the directions. Write the letter of the building.

_____ 1. Go up Park Avenue to the first traffic light. Turn right and go two blocks. Turn left and go to the end of the block. What is on the corner on the right?

_____ 2. Go up Park Avenue to First Street. Turn right and go one block. Turn left on Main Street. Then go one more block and turn right. What's on the left in the middle of the block?

_____ 3. Go straight on Park Avenue for three blocks. Turn right and go along Third Street. Go two blocks. What is on the left?

_____ 4. Go up Park Avenue to First Street. Turn right and go three blocks. What is on your left?

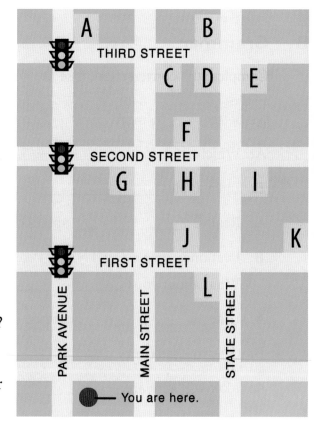

Check your English

Unit 9

A Vocabulary

Match the words with their meanings.

1. yoga ___

2. boxing ___

3. chess ___

4. comic book ___

5. guitar ___

6. table tennis ___

7. stamps ___

8. weights ___

a. Two people hit a small ball in this indoor sport.

b. You can play music with this.

c. This is a magazine with pictures that tell a story.

d. This is a difficult board game with 64 squares and 32 pieces.

e. People lift these heavy things.

f. This type of exercise is like stretching.

g. This is a fighting sport.

h. These are small pieces of paper we put on letters. Some people collect them.

B Grammar

Put the words in order to make sentences.

1. (go / to / snowboarding / do / like / you)

_____?

2. (snowboarding / do / weekend / want / go / to / you / this)

_____?

3. (to / what / you / free time / like / do / in / do / your)

_____?

4. (things / collect / like / I / to)

_____.

5. (like / you / things / do / what / to / kind / of / collect)

_____?

Check your English

Unit 10

A   Vocabulary

Complete the definitions. Use the words below.

take a cruise	flight	guidebook	change
tour	pack	reserve	beach

1. a book for travelers with information about a place = a _____

2. travel on a large boat to interesting places = _____

3. a trip in a bus to interesting places = a bus _____

4. put clothes in a suitcase = _____

5. save a seat on an airplane = book a _____

6. tell a hotel to keep a room for you = _____ a hotel room

7. give some money to get another type of money = _____ some money

8. go to a nice place to swim and lie in the sun = go to the _____

B   Grammar

Circle the words that correctly complete the conversations.

Conversation A

A: How was your trip to Mexico?

B: Great! I like / would like to go again.

A: Did you speak Spanish in Mexico?

B: All the time. I really like / would like
   to speak Spanish.

A: Is your Spanish very good?

B: It's OK. I like / would like to speak
   it better. Do you speak Spanish?

A: No, I don't. But I like / would like
   to learn it.

Conversation B

A: What are your travel plans?

B: I'll / I'm going to go backpacking.

A: When are you leaving?

B: I'm not sure. I'll / I'm going to probably
   leave in June.

A: Where are you going to go?

B: I don't know. I think I'll / I'm going to
   visit Thailand, but I'm not sure.

Check your English

Unit 11

A Vocabulary

Write the correct word under each picture. Use the words and phrases below.

add	bowl	box	can
pour	slice	turn on	wash

1. The cookies are in a _____.

2. Please _____ the microwave.

3. He's eating a _____ of cereal.

4. You should _____ the sauce over the fish.

5. This is a _____ of soup.

6. She has a _____ of pie.

7. _____ some salt.

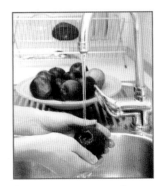

8. _____ the apple.

B Grammar

This is a recipe for apple banana soup. Number the sentences in the correct order from 1 to 6.

___ **a.** Finally, eat the soup.

___ **b.** Then, add 1 cup of yogurt to the orange juice.

___ **c.** First, pour 4 cups of orange juice into a bowl.

_1_ **d.** It's very easy to make fruit soup. This is how to make it.

___ **e.** After that, stir the yogurt, orange juice, and fruit slices with a large spoon.

___ **f.** Next, add 10 slices of apple and 10 slices of banana to the yogurt and orange juice.

Check your English

Unit 12

A Vocabulary

Complete the sentences. Use the words below.

build	truck	interview	care	direct
draw	write	language	dance	cook

1. My father knows how to drive a _____ .

2. I know you speak English. Can you speak another _____ ?

3. My brother knows how to _____ houses.

4. Listen to the beautiful music! Do you want to _____ with me?

5. Take this pencil and paper. Now, _____ a picture for me.

6. I don't know how to _____ a business letter. Can you help me?

7. Please come to my house for dinner. I can _____ very well.

8. I want Steven Spielberg's job—I want to _____ movies!

9. My mother works every day, so I take _____ of my little brother.

10. I can't _____ people because I don't like to ask questions.

B Grammar

Complete the questions. Use the words and phrases below. Then match questions 1 to 6 with answers a to f.

can	could	how well
know how	what	who

___ 1. What do you _____ to do?

___ 2. _____ can you drive?

___ 3. _____ can speak three languages?

___ 4. _____ he sing very well?

___ 5. _____ does she know how to cook?

___ 6. _____ Polly play the piano when she was seven?

a. Not very well.

b. Wei can.

c. Yes, she could.

d. I know how to cook.

e. Hamburgers and hot dogs.

f. No, he can't.

Key vocabulary

Here is a list of most of the new words in *Talk Time 2*.

adj = adjective
adv = adverb
n = noun
prep = preposition
pron = pronoun
v = verb

Unit 1

accountant *n*
actor *n*
airline *n*
airplane *n*
architect *n*
art history *n*
attend class *v*

chef *n*
company *n*
computer programmer *n*
computer science *n*

daily *adj, adv*
dentist *n*

go for a walk *v*

have lunch *v*
hobby *n*

international *adj*

job *n*

major *n*
musician *n*

orchestra *n*

pilot *n*
play sports *v*

salesperson *n*
Singapore *n*
surf the Internet *v*

take the subway *v*
teacher *n*
tour guide *n*

web designer *n*
What do you do?

Unit 2

angry *adj*
bored *adj*

classmate *n*
current *adj*

day *n*

excited *adj*

feelings *n*
full-time *adj*

happen *v*
happy *adj*
have something in common *idiom*

live at home *v*

nervous *adj*

part-time *adj*

semester *n*
still *adv*
study Chinese *v*
surprised *adj*

take a class *v*
teach at a university *v*

visit one's family *v*

work in a restaurant *v*
write a paper *v*

Unit 3

admire *v*
artist *n*

beautiful *adj*

charming *adj*
city *n*

clean *adj*
crowded *adj*

die *v*
Dutch *adj, n*

English *adj, n*
excellent *adj*
exciting *adj*
expensive *adj*

fascinating *adj*
friendly *adj*

hectic *adj*
historic *adj*

interesting *adj*
inventor *n*
Italian *adj, n*

Japanese *adj, n*

Kuala Lumpur *n*

leader *n*
learn *v*

modern *adj*
movie director *n*

noisy *adj*

old *adj*

people *n*
pleasant *adj*
Polish *adj*

queen *n*
quiet *adj*

romantic *adj*

safe *adj*
scientist *n*
small *adj*

weather *n*
writer *n*

Unit 4

barbecue   *n*

drive somewhere   *v*

get together with friends   *v*
get up late   *v*
go camping   *v*
go sightseeing   *v*

have dinner in a restaurant   *v*

karaoke club   *n*

meet friends   *v*
meet someone new   *v*

order a pizza   *v*

play computer games   *v*

read a book   *v*
rock climbing   *n*

see a movie   *v*
spend (time)   *v*
stay home   *v*

take a nap   *v*

visit museums   *v*
visit parents   *v*

watch DVDs   *v*
weekend   *n*
work   *v*

Unit 5

baseball game   *n*
by the way...

cafe   *n*
classical   *n*
concert   *n*
country and western   *n*

dance club   *n*
dance performance   *n*

entertainment   *n*

golf tournament   *n*

hip-hop   *n*
how about...?

jazz   *n*

let's...   *v*

museum   *n*

opera   *n*

park   *n*
picnic   *n*
play   *n*
pop   *n*

rock   *n*

soccer match   *n*

ticket   *n*

what about...?

zoo   *n*

Unit 6

across from   *prep*
ATM (automated teller
machine)   *n*

behind   *prep*
between   *prep*
bus stop   *n*
bus   *n*

change   *n*
city square   *n*
clothes   *n pl*
coffee shop   *n*
color   *n*
conductor   *n*

driver   *n*
drugstore   *n*

Excuse me.

fare   *n*
free   *adj*

hotel   *n*

in front of   *prep*

library   *n*
lost   *adj*

mailbox   *n*
movie theater   *n*
museum   *n*

near   *prep*
newsstand   *n*
next to   *prep*

on the corner of   *prep*
on   *prep*

park   *n*
parking lot   *n*
passenger   *n*
platform   *n*
post office   *n*
public transportation   *n*

station   *n*

taxi stand   *n*
taxi   *n*
ticket machine   *n*
ticket   *n*
train   *n*

Unit 7

a few   *pron*
a little   *pron*
any   *pron*
apple   *n*

banana   *n*
beef   *n*
better   *adj*
blue jeans   *n pl*
boots   *n*
butter   *n*

cap   *n*
carrot   *n*
cheese   *n*

chicken   *n*
coat   *n*
corn   *n*

dress   *n*

egg   *n*

fish   *n*

jacket   *n*
juice   *n*

milk   *n*

need   *v*
none   *pron*

one   *pron*
orange   *n*

pants   *n pl*
potato   *n*

scarf   *n*
shirt   *n*
shoes   *n pl*
shopping list   *n*
skirt   *n*
sneakers   *n pl*
sock   *n*
some   *pron*
supermarket   *n*
sweater   *n*

tie   *n*
That's all.
tofu   *n*
tomato   *n*
too   *adv*
T-shirt   *n*

Unit 8

across   *prep*
along   *prep*
around   *prep*

bakery   *n*
bank   *n*
block   *n*

bookstore   *n*
bridge   *n*

city hall/town hall   *n*
clothing store   *n*

fire station   *n*
furniture store   *n*

gas station   *n*
go up   *v*

hair salon   *n*
hospital   *n*

ice cream shop   *n*

jewelry store   *n*

music store   *n*

on the right/left   *prep*
over   *prep*

past   *prep*
pet store   *n*
pizza place   *n*
place   *n*
police station   *n*
pond   *n*

river   *n*

shoe store   *n*
shop   *n*
shopping mall   *n*
sporting goods store   *n*
stadium   *n*
stationery store   *n*
straight   *prep*

through   *prep*
town   *n*
tunnel   *n*
turn right/left   *v*

under   *prep*

video store   *n*

Unit 9

be in (good) shape   *v*
be interested in   *v*
board games   *n*
box   *v*

can't stand   *v*
caps   *n pl*
cards   *n pl*
chess   *n pl*
comic books   *n pl*

decide   *v*
do judo   *v*
do puzzles   *v*
do yoga   *v*
don't like   *v*

enjoy   *v*
exercise   *n*

guitar   *n*

hate   *v*

indoor   *adj*

lift weights   *v*
like   *v*
love   *v*

paint   *v*
plan   *v*
play table tennis   *v*
prefer   *v*

stamps   *n*
surf the Internet   *v*

trading cards   *n*

wrestle   *v*

Unit 10

apply for a visa   *v*

backpacking   *n*
book   *v*
bus tour   *n*

buy   *v*
by   *adv*

change some money   *v*
cruise   *n*

flight   *n*

guidebook   *n*
guided tour   *n*

hotel room   *n*

of course

pack   *v*
preparation   *n*
probably   *adv*

rafting   *n*
reserve   *v*

Switzerland   *n*

take   *v*
train trip   *n*

white-water rafting   *n*

Unit 11

add   *v*
after that   *adv*

bag   *n*
bake   *v*
baked   *adj*
beans   *n pl*
boil   *v*
bottle   *n*
bowl   *n*
box   *n*
bread   *n*

can   *n*
carton   *n*
checkout counter   *n*
chop   *v*
container   *n*
cup   *n*

drink   *v*

easy   *adj*

finally   *adv*
first   *adv*
fry   *v*

glass   *n*

iced tea   *n*

jar   *n*

loaf   *n*

microwave (oven)   *n*

next   *adv*

order   *v*

peel   *v*
plate   *n*
pour   *v*
put in   *v*

quantity   *n*

rice   *n*

show   *v*
six-pack   *n*
slice   *n, v*
spoonful   *n*
stir   *v*
sugar   *n*

turn on   *v*

wash   *v*

Unit 12

artistic   *adj*
act   *v*

build houses   *v*

child   *n*
cook   *v*

dance   *v*
design web pages   *v*
direct movies   *v*
draw   *v*

drive a truck   *v*

interview people   *v*

kid   *n* (informal)

repair computers   *v*

sell   *v*
sing   *v*
skill   *n*
speak another language   *v*

take care of children   *v*
talent   *n*
teach   *v*

use a computer   *v*

write business letters   *v*
write music   *v*